TROY DANN'S
OUTBACK

WILD ADVENTURES FOR THE WHOLE FAMILY

RANDOM HOUSE AUSTRALIA

Random House Australia Pty Ltd
20 Alfred Street, Milsons Point NSW 2061
fax: 612 9955 3381
http://www.randomhouse.com.au

Sydney New York Toronto London Auckland Johannesburg
and agencies throughout the world

First published in 2000
© Troy Dann
© Photographs Random House Photo Library and others
(for full list, see page 126)

National Library of Australia Cataloguing-in-Publication data

Dann, Troy.
Troy Dann's outback: wild adventures for the whole family.

ISBN 1 74051 709 1.

1. Dann, Troy. 2. Zoology - Northern Territory. 3. Country life -
Northern territory. 4. Northern Territory - Description and travel.
I. Title.

919.429

Children's Publisher: Linsay Knight
Managing Editor: Loretta Barnard
Designer: Liz Seymour
Additional writing: Marli Kelly, Loretta Barnard
Picture research: Loretta Barnard
Photo Librarian: Susan Page
Publishing Coordinator: Pia Gerard
Production Manager: Lisa Hanrahan

Colour separation by Response Colour Graphics, Sydney
Printed by Phoenix, Hong Kong

CONTENTS

INTRODUCTION

With my uncle Scottie.

When people think about the Australian Outback, they think of the rich red colours of the desert, and the crystal clear blue of the skies and there's no doubt that the colours of the landscape are uniquely Australian. When I travel around the world, I'm often asked to compare the Australian outback with other parts of the world. I can't do it! There is no comparison, and while there are many spectacularly beautiful places around the globe, there's nothing that can match the grandeur of the Australian Outback.

I was born in the bush, so a deep love and respect for the land is part of my make-up. I also feel passionate about sharing this love, especially with young people. In these days of the so-called 'global village', it's easy to lose sight of your own heritage. It's important to me to keep our heritage alive and to pass down our traditions and our culture to future generations.

I can't cover everything I'd like to in a book this size, so I've tried to introduce you to just some aspects of Australian bush culture. I hope this whets your appetite for more!

Preparing for a cattle muster.

ACKNOWLEDGEMENTS

Thank you to all the people who helped me put this book together.

Marli Kelly, thanks for your hard work and excellent research towards writing this book, and for keeping on my back to get it finished. You're a great friend.

Belinda Jakiel, Lynne Kelly and the Ditterich Family, all of whom who assisted in various ways with the research. Thank you.

Belinda Williams, thanks for helping with the chapter on Outback artists.

Michael McGennan, thanks again mate.

Bill Leimbach, thanks for your help and support.

Mum and Dad, thanks for everything. Your support means the world to me.

My sisters, Simone, Tanya and Heidi, love you.

My girl Sarah, thanks honey, love you.

Thanks also to all the generous people who allowed us to use photographs and illustrations for the book.

To all the staff at Random House, especially Linsay Knight and Loretta Barnard, you are wonderful. Thanks for your great work.

CHAPTER 1
FERAL ANIMALS

Australia has been a largely isolated continent, and for millions of years plants and animals here adapted to life in this isolation. With European settlement however, a number of animals were introduced, resulting in some immeasurable effects on the Australian environment.

Introduced species have contributed to the extinction of up to 40 species of Australian animals and nearly 70 species of Australian plants.

'Feral' says it all! Feral animals are those which have been introduced from another country and have adapted to Australian habitats in the wild. Their adaptation, growth and impact has been largely uncontrolled by humans.

Feral animals create a number of problems for the environment. They compete with native species for food, shelter and nesting sites. Some of the major environmental issues are the impact on our native animals' lifestyle and survival, occurrence of attacks on native species, maiming, and the possibility of spreading disease among wildlife.

This chapter explores some of the feral species now running wild in Australia:

- camels
- donkeys
- foxes
- rabbits
- cats
- cane toads
- dingoes
- buffaloes
- pigs
- brumbies

How can you help?
To help our native flora and fauna survive, you could plant a native tree in your garden to attract bird life. Spell (or rest) your paddocks so that they are not overstocked. Plant grass in eroded areas to protect the soil. There are many ways to preserve the land, and as we are lucky enough to live in this big beautiful country, we need to respect her. We do not own Mother Earth, and we should all do our bit to help preserve it where possible.

Sometimes you have to be cruel to be kind. This means that some introduced animals must be culled, to give a fair chance of survival for native species.

Feral goats eat almost any kind of vegetation. These highly adaptable animals survive very well in the Outback.

CAMELS

TROY'S TIP

Camels seem to
have universal joints
in their knee caps
as they can kick
you from any direction.
So watch out!

There are millions of camels all around the world. But by a trick of history, a small matter of the local environment, and a good dose of luck, the wild-running camels of Australia are the healthiest on the planet. All two or three hundred thousand of them. We have about 500 domesticated camels living on our property in Central Australia. The first camels were brought here, along with their mostly Afghan handlers, some 150 years ago.

They were used on the Burke and Wills expedition from Adelaide to the far north coast and back. Who's to say whether one of the great-granddaddies of the current wild flock may not have been the last living thing the dying explorers ever saw?

Following on from the explorers, camels were used as beasts of burden by miners, telegraph-line builders (including my great-grandparents and great-uncles), surveyors and tradesmen all over the Outback. The camel was a four-footed pioneer of Central Australia.

A mature beast would casually put in an 8–10 hour working day carrying packs weighing anything up to 300 kilograms over a distance of 30 kilometres or more. But as mechanised vehicles were introduced early in the twentieth century, and finally took over the brute tasks of transportation, camels were let loose all over the country.

Out on their own, moving in often quite large groups, the camels then (and still) thrived on native vegetation. Best of all, what they eat and the way they eat it—never entirely clearing an area of fodder, nor tearing plants right out of the ground, as sheep and cattle can do at times—the camels have not threatened the existence of either native or domestic animals in the areas they share. In fact, there's some evidence that cattle browsing the same areas as camels have actually picked up a microscopic bug that used to live exclusively in the camels' stomachs. Now resident in cattle as well, it's offering natural protection against a range of potential diseases, and helps to break down roughage and grasses.

DID YOU KNOW ... The male camel is the one that comes on heat, not the female. They get very aggressive and will spit at you if provoked. And let me tell you they don't smell pretty.

Camels' fleshy humps contain stored fat they can draw on for sustenance. They also manufacture water by the oxidation of this fat. They lose their body water slowly and might shed up to 25 per cent of their body weight by dehydration without ill effects. Perhaps this is because camels know they'll easily regain that lost weight by their remarkable ability to drink as much as 100 litres (25 gallons) of water in a few minutes. That long neck also allows it to nibble on vegetation too high for other animals to reach, in the branches of many native trees.

Among the other desert-specific advantages camels have is the size of their feet. As broad as 25 centimetres on a mature animal, the cushioned pad gives a camel stability in loose sand. This photo was taken on the shores of the Great Australian Bight.

A camel's nose, with narrow slit-like nostrils, thickly lined with hairs, can close tight to keep out dust and sand. Their eyes are protected by overhanging brows and heavy, long-lashed eyelids.

The camels of Outback Australia are perfectly suited to endure harsh conditions. They would certainly have easily survived here for thousands of years if they'd been native to the continent. They are such intelligent animals and to me, the land and environment is better off for it!

This is me on a camel. My great-uncle, Ted Colson, was the first white man to cross the Simpson Desert by camel, so riding camels is in my blood!

DONKEYS

Donkeys were introduced to Australia by European settlers as pack and draught animals. They could carry heavy loads, and were often used on expeditions instead of horses because of their ability to handle the dry and rough terrain. My own ancestors used them back in the early days, when helping to open up outback Australia. Donkeys were easy to maintain—they required little to drink and could feed from the surrounding bush land, which sometimes became very marginal.

With the introduction of machinery and motorised transport such as the car and truck, many donkeys were set free. These became feral. Donkeys, which are usually coloured black and grey, group in herds of approximately 30, but during dry periods can be found in herds of several hundred. They are found in central Australia and parts of central Queensland, but mainly in northwest Western Australia. The Kimberley region is home to the largest feral donkey population in the country.

Feral donkeys are found mainly in the flats of major river and creek systems, an environment similar to the one where you'd find cattle. These locations ensure good grazing and adequate sources of water.

My family once owned a property called Mistake Creek near the Kimberleys and flying around it in our *Cessna 182* I would see hundreds of these animals. We must have had around 5,000 of them at one stage. In order to look after the environment, the government has since culled them down, but there are still hundreds of thousands of them in the wild. In fact, the current population of donkeys in Australia is estimated to be between one and two million!

FOXES

Foxes were supposedly introduced into Australia as early as the 1840s. They say the first successful release occurred in 1855 in southern Victoria near Melbourne. This introduction provided two things. One was fox hunting (for sport); the other was to address the problem created by the rapid increase in the rabbit population. Next to the dingo, the fox is the largest land carnivore in Australia, but the fox is very much a pest.

I've only seen the odd fox in the Northern Territory, but foxes do occur throughout much of Australia, apart from Tasmania. Foxes can also be seen in the outskirts of several Australian cities. Because of their adaptability, they can exist in a range of habitats from alpine to urban Australia. They are very successful introduced animals. They breed once a year and have a life expectancy of approximately four years.

Like many other feral animals, foxes have had numerous effects on the native environment. Certain species of native wildlife have been truly adversely affected—foxes are the main reason why numbats and black-flanked rock wallabies are close to extinction. Foxes also eat quolls, possums and bandicoots, threatening extinction to them all.

The agricultural industry also suffers. Foxes prey on newborn lambs, chickens, ducks, geese, calves and the odd goat kid. Farmers find them a real pest. As well as native animals and livestock, foxes eat mice, carrion and rabbits, not to mention food scraps from garbage bins.

Another risk posed by foxes is that they are potential carriers of rabies. This disease mostly affects dogs, but it can be passed to humans, livestock and native mammals.

Controlling the impact of foxes is currently managed through shooting and poisoning, although in the future it is hoped that biological control can be used—together with these conventional methods—to control numbers.

DID YOU KNOW ... Governments once paid a bounty (money) to hunters, pastoralists and farmers for every fox killed in order to eliminate them. Fox skins are still sold today to make fur coats.

RABBITS

The bunny rabbit—another nightmare in the Australian outback! Luckily, we don't have many rabbits on Amburla, but I remember growing up on my family's property, Waite River, 250 kilometres northeast of Alice Springs, where there were thousands of them. I'll never forget the time my dad bought me a ferret (a horrible little creature with sharp teeth). The idea was to put the ferret down a rabbit warren to chase the rabbits out. A net was put over the hole so you could catch them as they came running out. Early one morning we found a good set of burrows, but there were 13 holes and only 12 nets. Thinking I would be smart, I picked out the oldest looking hole. I left it free of a net as it had obviously not been used for some time. After placing the 12 nets over the holes, I excitedly let the ferret out of its bag and into the hole … I waited in anticipation for around five minutes when you wouldn't believe it, not one, but two, rabbits came bouncing out! Where did they came out? That old hole, the only hole without a net. Off they went out of sight! On top of that we waited for a good hour or two for the ferret to surface, but you know he never came out. That was the end of my rabbit trapping days. I was not very good at it!

Although domestic rabbits arrived with the first fleet of ships in Australia, wild rabbits were first introduced into Australia in 1859 as game. Originally, so I'm told, 24 rabbits were brought from England to Victoria. Today they've spread everywhere, with roughly over 300 million found throughout Australia.

Rabbits have had a major environmental and agricultural effect on our nation. Rabbits are grazers but will browse when grasses are scarce, eating seedlings of native plants. This prevents the plants from regenerating. Rabbits also select the most nutritious plants and eat them below ground level. When an area is overgrazed it loses plant cover, causing erosion.

Agricultural production is affected by rabbits. It is worse in drier areas where pasture production is low. When rabbit numbers increase, they compete with livestock for pasture food. This makes them a true pest to agriculture.

The management of rabbits is of real concern to farmers and land managers alike. The release of myxomatosis in 1950 was very successful at reducing rabbit numbers and in the six months following the release, the virus was believed to have killed more than 90 per cent of rabbits. How our nation chooses to deal with the problem continues to be explored through research studies. We really do need to address the impact these animals are having on Australia.

CATS

European settlement confirms the arrival of cats as domestic pets, yet many believe that they may have come earlier than this, with the Dutch explorers, some of whose ships were wrecked in Australian waters in the seventeenth century. In the late 1800s, cats were introduced with the aim of controlling the large numbers of rabbits, rats and mice. Of course, since then they have spread, and now cover the entire country.

It would have been alright if they were kept as domestic cats in a family home, but seeing what these feral creatures have done to our native wildlife makes me wild! They are so destructive. There are countless examples of feral cats directly affecting endangered and other native species, and they are responsible for the extinction of some small mammals.

The other thing that makes me angry is the number of beautiful birds they eat. When I go around Amburla on a bore run checking our waters for the stock, I often see the remains of a parrot or some other species that has been attacked by a feral cat. All that's left is a lot of feathers. If a cat could digest the feathers I'd reckon they'd eat them as well. Seems nothing is sacred to a cat in the wild.

The feral cat is an adaptable animal; it can survive almost anywhere. It can live in both wet and dry conditions. In very dry conditions, it survives by living off the moisture of its prey.

Addressing the impact feral cats have on our country involves using a number of methods. These include baiting, fencing, trapping and shooting. Unfortunately, eradication from the mainland is almost impossible.

Studies which aim to understand the impact feral cats have on the native wildlife are ongoing. We taxpayers are paying for it year after year. But to me, the main study has already been done over many years by experienced pastoralists and farmers. The solution is not rocket science, just common sense—bait them extensively to really cull their numbers down. People on the land, who care about our environment and the well-being of native animals and birds, know this is the answer. Now I'm not talking about a family cat in an urban area which may be straying. I'm saying that in the wide open spaces of the outback, many animals and reptiles are working hard to survive—they don't need the added burden of being hunted by the feral cat!

DID YOU KNOW ... A cat hunts mainly at night sneaking up on its prey with lightning reflexes and amazing eyesight!

CANE TOADS

I think these little critters are little menaces! In 1935, the cane toad was introduced to the sugar cane fields in Queensland in an effort to control cane beetles, a real pest problem. Unfortunately, the effort was unsuccessful, and the toad quickly adapted to its new home, rapidly spreading throughout Queensland, northern New South Wales and now my home state, the Northern Territory. Cane toads are olive-brown to reddish brown on top, with a belly of pale white or yellow. They can survive in almost all environments except freezing conditions, and need to live near water.

The success of the cane toad in Australia is due to a number of factors. One is its adaptability to a range of habitats. Another is its very effective reproductive rate. As well, the toad has very few natural predators in Australia. Among its predators are keelback snakes, water rats, ibis, crows, freshwater snakes and crocodiles. In the early days, however, many of these animals and birds fell victim to the cane toad's toxic venom, but over time, they learned how to eat them without getting poisoned.

In the summer of 1998, I was travelling up the Lemmon Bite River in the Gulf of Carpentaria. I was in a dinghy with some mates heading out to catch a few fish, when the smell of dead flesh hit our nostrils. To our astonishment, we saw about six dead freshwater crocodiles—all bloated up—on the edge of the bank. I knew it couldn't be hunters, because the hides would have been skinned; and these creatures are prehistoric—they've outlived dinosaurs and the Ice Age, what could possibly have killed them? They have no predators except for man's gun. Then the penny dropped. Hopping all round these waters were hundreds of these wretched cane toads. They had finally made it halfway between Queensland and Darwin, the capital city of the Northern Territory. I bet it won't be long until freshwater crocodiles work out that they should stay clear of the cane toad.

Cane toads have large appetites, so they have a real effect on native ground-dwelling micro-fauna. Their primary food is insects, and they also eat small lizards, mice, frogs and even younger cane toads.

There is a lot of work to be done on the effect cane toads are having on native wildlife, as well as how far they have spread. Cane toads provide a painful lesson about what can happen to our precious native species when introduced animals or plants are allowed into a new habitat.

DINGOES

The dingo is Australia's native dog. Its origins are unknown and there are many contrasting views; however, it is thought that approximately 40,000 years ago, when the Aboriginal people came to Australia, they brought the dingo with them. It is believed to have originated in Asia, possibly Thailand, as a wild dog. I find this very believable because on the few occasions I've been in Asia, I noticed that all their pet dogs were dingoes.

Dingoes and dogs are members of the same species and are able to inter-breed, but dingoes have bigger teeth, a narrower snout, brushier tail, and broader feet.

Dingoes are found all around Australia, except Tasmania, living in woodlands, forests and open grass lands where they have access to drinking water. They breed up in the hills on our property and sometimes their numbers are so great that it's necessary to bait them to keep their numbers down. If we don't take these measures, they will try to eat our Brahman calves.

It is only when they are in packs that dingoes will try to take a bigger animal, but on their own, my view is that they are quite timid scavengers. Either in a family group or roaming alone, dingoes feed on a range of foods, mainly rats, mice, kangaroos, wallabies, lizards and fruit. Mammals usually comprise about two-thirds of their diet. They are intelligent and to see them work in a pack hunting down their prey is amazing.

Dingoes are not a big threat to the Australian habitat, although farmers are aware that they do attack sheep and smaller farm animals. The longest fence in the world was erected in an attempt to keep dingoes off grazing lands in southeastern Australia.

Dingoes only breed once a year, unlike dogs, which can breed twice a year. Birth is usually two months after mating, and anything from one to eight pups are born. At two weeks of age, the pups feed on regurgitated meat as well as their mother's milk. Pups remain dependent on the mother until they are about six months old. I love dingo pups—they are so cuddly.

Pure breed numbers are decreasing in the wild, and many dingoes are being domesticated. As long as their numbers are controlled, I say 'long live the dingo'.

DID YOU KNOW ... Dingoes cannot bark and instead they howl. Howling is used for locating mates, calling pups and defining territory.

BUFFALOES

The water buffalo was introduced into the Top End of Australia from the eastern islands of the Indonesian Archipelago in the 1820s. With its tropical climate, broad wetlands, lush grass and other vegetation of the northern swamps and lagoons, this is the only area they can really thrive.

Pastoralists knew that buffalo, especially those under domestication, provided good milk, palatable flesh, and a skin which could be made into high-quality leather. Since British and European cattle did not thrive in the tropics, these clear advantages led to more of these animals being introduced over the ensuing decades. They can cope with hot temperatures by wallowing in mud holes and water and sheltering under dense vegetation.

While the buffalo has become something of a symbol of the Northern Territory, the unfortunate reality is that, outside stations running domesticated animals, and the herds contained in game parks, free-ranging buffaloes do a lot of damage to the environment. This damage compromises the land itself, the survival of the wetlands, and the lives of many native species of flora and fauna. Skimming around in an airboat (what a blast!) across the floodplains of the north, I have seen these problems first hand. Now, however, thanks to fellow pastoralists and the Conservation Commission, they are coming under control.

The main problem is their sheer size. A mature male can measure 2.5 to 3 metres, nose to tail, and easily weigh in at 700 to 800 kilograms, some even heavier.

By the dry season's end the feral herds have either trampled on or grazed off most of the vegetation on the grassy plains and swamps they congregate in. After daily wallows in waterholes and billabongs, they leave behind not much more than muddy puddles. Their paths away erode channels and gullies in the natural levees. This often allows salt water to break through into the swampy plains, killing many plants and making the water undrinkable.

In forested areas, buffaloes eat young trees and shrubs, eliminating opportunities for much vitally necessary regeneration. Such destruction of the vegetation also makes the habitat unsuitable for native animals, and compromises their survival. Yet, if properly controlled, the buffalo can provide good export money to the economy of Australia, and can go on being the symbol of a vital, strong Northern Territory.

TROY'S TIP

Don't underestimate the speed of a wild buffalo cow. She can run a lot faster than you or I, especially when she has a young calf at foot. She won't hesitate to horn you as she is so protective of her young.

DID YOU KNOW ... A buffalo's judgment is so accurate that if you throw a fifty cent coin at a buffalo, it can hit the coin with the tip of its horn!

PIGS

If there is any animal in Australia that is an agricultural pest and super-destructive to our environment, it is the feral pig! Pigs were introduced from Europe and Asia into Australia to be hunted for food. Feral populations were soon established when insufficient enclosures and deliberate releases sent pigs roaming throughout much of the country. And they reproduce quickly: a mature female often rears two litters in a year. There are now feral pigs in every state of Australia except Tasmania.

Feral pigs cause immeasurable damage to the native environment. They are nocturnal animals with most activity around dawn and dusk. They feed on natural flora, as well as roots, grain crops, berries and fruit, frogs, lizards, small to medium-sized vertebrates and carrion. The night's activity usually begins with a big wallow in a muddy pool, and this is one of the ways pigs damage the environment—plants growing in and at the edges of these pools are destroyed. This not only causes erosion, it removes feeding and nesting sites for native animals.

Feral pigs need to drink daily in hot weather, so they are not often found in dry inland areas where there is no permanent surface water. Wherever I travel in the wet parts of the outback all over Australia, I see a trail of destruction from these pests—from the floodplains of the Top End to the tropics across the channel country of Queensland.

Yet another hazard posed by the feral pig is its potential to carry disease and parasites. These could be transmitted to humans, native animals and domestic livestock alike. The biggest concern is the transmission of 'foot-and-mouth' disease.

Pig hunters and pastoralists are doing a good job to help the environment by culling them, and dogs are of enormous assistance in this process. They help their owners hunt down the pigs by smelling them out and catching them. This can be a dangerous task if you don't know what you're doing! The dogs love their work, and they're also doing a great job for their owners and their country. Yet feral pigs, like other pests, remain widespread, and despite the best efforts of governments and land-owners, their presence is a national problem.

TROY'S TIP

A sow can get very cranky when protecting her young and will attack you quick smart. My advice if you see her coarse mane bristle is to get out of the way, because she will seriously hurt you. Leave it to professionals to hunt and catch them.

Chasing a wild pig. It's really quite tricky!

BRUMBIES

This is a photo of a wild brumby running with our station work horses. You can tell the brumby by its long boom tail and long mane.

The Australian wild horse is known to Aboriginal people as the 'brumby'. Like most of the animals listed as feral in this country, the brumby has really only roamed the continent since the arrival of Europeans in the late 1780s. These horses escaped from our forefathers' farms and cattle properties into the wild unknown. Today, wild horses can be found from the steep and snowy ranges of the southeast in Victoria and New South Wales, to the harshly arid Red Centre of the continent. They come in varied colours and are beautiful animals to watch.

Not many people know that brumbies made a substantial contribution to world history. During the two world wars, many of them were rounded up and

shipped overseas, alongside domesticated horses, to be used as cavalry mounts.

Most prized were the 'Walers', which were particularly strong horses that could work all day in the toughest of conditions. Why 'Walers'? Their name as a locally bred workhorse traced back to the time when all of Australia was called New South Wales. The breeding ground for these Walers is not far from my home in the Western MacDonnell Ranges.

Because of their large numbers, brumbies have been a threat to the environment. They compete with native animals and domestic beasts for scarce water and fodder supplies. Erosion of the land is another result of their presence. Because the centre of the country is now a national park, it has been necessary to cull thousands of these magnificent animals in the last decade or so, to keep erosion to a minimum. Another reason for culling brumbies is to allow the other living creatures in the same area a chance to survive.

But riding around on my own horse, I have learnt that the brumby can be of assistance to other animals in such tough times as protracted drought. A brumby uses its hooves to dig down to water at the bottom of a dry creek bed, leaving access to that same water for other creatures after it has moved on.

Nowadays, there are many water supplies in outback Australia, so I'm pleased to say that brumbies will never be threated with extinction and will always roam our lucky country. They are no doubt among my favourite creatures.

CHAPTER 2

NATIVE ANIMALS

For some 60 million years, the life forms in Australia evolved in splendid isolation from the rest of the earth's landmasses. Set apart and surrounded by ocean, animal life developed some bizarre attributes. From the egg-laying mammalian platypus to gastric-brooding frogs, from frilled lizards to jumping joeys, an amazing variety of lizards and snakes came to be. Scientists are still learning much about our native animals. I wonder if we'll ever know all we can about these wonderful creatures?

Coming into contact with some of our native wildlife is a magical experience for many people and it's great when you can share that experience with friends and visitors from other lands.

But contact with people has not always produced the best results for animals. During the last two centuries in Australia, there has been a decrease in many animal species. The causes for this decline include habitat destruction, introduced animals and plants, the use of pesticides and fertilisers, pollution and the impact of motor vehicles. Australia has lost more mammal species than any other country in the world.

This chapter explores some of our more colourful Australian animals. From the national icons of the koala and kangaroo to the majestic perentie, you'll discover some of the amazing habits these animals have and how they have adapted to life in in this often harsh but beautiful country.

The thorny devil is one of the Northern Territory's more unusual looking reptiles. This little bloke only grows to a length of 15 centimetres.

EURO

The euro has quite a distinctive appearance. It is a large, stocky marsupial with shaggy fur and a stiff, upright posture when hopping. It is most commonly seen in rocky hills, where it shelters in crevices and caves during the day, emerging to feed only in the cool of the evening. I love flying my helicopter through the hills in the outback trying to spot euros. I have this old euro mate I've nicknamed Bob. I see him a few times a year on the top of one of our hills at Amburla. Six months ago I noticed that one of his ears was missing, and that he was looking a bit battered and bruised—he had obviously got into a fight with another male. He must've won because he still had the girl, a beautiful young doe alongside him. I'd hate to see what the other bloke looked like if Bob had come off better!

RED-NECKED WALLABY

Red-necked wallabies are found in the forest areas of southeastern Australia. They look like someone took to them with a paint brush, colouring their necks and upper limbs rust red. Red-necked wallabies differ from larger kangaroos in that they don't like to be surrounded by their whole community. They are happy to stay in small family groups, sheltering in the forest during the day and emerging at dusk to take off on their moonlight adventures. I must have a bit of red-necked wallaby in me too, because I love adventures.

Unlike joeys from other kangaroo and wallaby groups who stay close to their mum after they leave the pouch, these wallaby joeys think they are way too cool to hang out with Mum, and hide and feed under cover while she feeds nearby. This is in spite of the fact that young joeys are prey for dingoes, foxes and eagles. Young males spend their time play-fighting and practising their boxing skills. They are preparing for when they are older and must compete with other males for mates.

RED KANGAROO

The image of a kangaroo bounding across the plains is synonymous with Australia. The kangaroo is on our coat of arms and on Qantas jets. Its name is believed to be Aboriginal in origin. The first European explorers asked the indigenous people what these strange animals were, and they answered 'kangaroo' meaning 'I don't understand'. The name stuck.

The red kangaroo is the world's largest living marsupial. It is found in abundance near my home in the Northern Territory. They are grazing animals, and are known to move up to 50 kilometres a night—that's quite a way just to fill up your tummy. Sometimes, however, kangaroos feed during the evening and early morning to obtain early morning dew from the grass. When water is available they will drink, but they don't need to if sufficient green food is eaten.

In hot conditions, the red kangaroo has a nap in the shade, conserving its energy for later. It licks its limbs, and the evaporating saliva cools it down. Its fur can also reflect heat. See how the kangaroo has adapted to the dry conditions of its home?

Its powerful hind legs and long hind feet allow the kangaroo to move with ease. When grazing, the kangaroo uses its tail in a five-pointed gait so the limbs move forward. When stationary, the tail acts as the kangaroo's own little stool that it can rest back on.

I find it amazing that in a good season they can have up to three young at one time. How's that, you say? Well, a big joey outside the pouch, a small one in the pouch, and an even smaller one as an embryo on its way! Red kangaroos are only about the size of a bumblebee at birth. Hairless and with no eyes, ears or tail they make their way to the mother's pouch where they spend approximately eight months. At the end of this period the young joey leaves its mother's pouch for short bursts, gradually testing his independence. After about nine months, the joey is pretty much independent, only sometimes drinking from a teat.

Grey and red kangaroos share the land and all it has to offer.

DID YOU KNOW ... When I've been chasing wild horses on my motor-bike, I've clocked red kangaroos at 60 kilometres per hour!

ECHIDNA

The echidna, like the platypus, caused havoc to early naturalists who were trying to work out how to classify them. They were confused because they were mammals that fed their young on milk, but laid eggs like reptiles. These remarkable animals are now classified as monotremes.

The echidna is also called the spiny anteater, and is known for the spikes covering its body. These spikes are actually hairs and are a defence mechanism against predators. Aboriginal people had a clever use for echidna spikes—they used them to help remove splinters. Sort of like bush needles.

The echidna is also famous for its ability to escape danger. If caught, it burrows down and in a matter of seconds all you see is a small tuft of its spine tips. Once it has burrowed into the soil it is very difficult to get out, so it is safe from harm. A pretty cool survival mechanism!

The echidna is toothless and feeds solely on ants and termites. With its snout and claws, it tunnels down into the earth extending its tongue downward into the ant or termite mound. Its tongue, which is up to 15 centimetres long, can move at lightning speeds. It is covered with thick saliva like treacle, and insects are stuck to the tongue and quickly transferred to the mouth. If it's feeling lazy, the echidna parks itself on top of an anthill and leaves its tongue hanging out to catch the ants that run across it.

Courting males run a contest among themselves to determine who gets to mate with the female. They follow the female Indian file in a procession for up to four weeks. The female chooses a place to burrow down and the males then dig trenches around her. This is when the fun starts and the males have a head to head shoving contest with the winner getting the girl. A good reason for the males to stay in shape! A single egg is laid in a temporary pouch, which develops at the onset of breeding. The egg hatches after about 10 days. The young echidna suckles the mother until its spines begin to develop, but stays with the mother in the burrow for another three months.

TROY'S TIP

The spines of the echidna are very sharp. A cut from one could result in bacterial infection, so handling echidnas is not a good idea!

PLATYPUS

Did you see Syd the Platypus as one of the mascots of the Sydney Olympic Games? Along with Millie the Echidna and Olly the Kookaburra, Syd got into lots of mischief and delighted everyone. It was fabulous to see three of our more unusual native animals representing Australia.

In 1798, the first platypus skin was taken back to England to be analysed, and the scientists studying it thought that someone was playing a joke on them. They couldn't believe that any animal could look like that. That original platypus skin still exists today and has scissor marks on it where a scientist tried to remove the beak. The unusual characteristics of many of our Australian animals have baffled the world's scientists.

The platypus is perhaps the best known monotreme, a mammal that lays eggs instead of giving birth to its young. It lives in freshwater rivers and lakes in eastern Australia. Its thick fur is like a wetsuit, trapping a layer of air next to the skin to protect it from the cold, while its flat tail and webbed feet help it to swim in water. As the platypus dives under water it closes its eyes, nostrils and ears and uses the touch receptors in the skin of the bill to help it navigate. The bill detects electrical impulses from movement in the water. It's like having an in-built radar system!

DID YOU KNOW ... Platypuses have no nipples. The female sweats the milk onto her belly.

The platypus usually feeds at night stirring up mud or silt on the bottom of rivers and lakes. It has a sensitive, flexible, duck-like snout. It collects food samples and stores them in its cheek pouches so that they can be chewed after returning to the surface.

Adult males have a spur on the inside of each hind leg. These connect to a venom gland that produces a strong toxin. Although it can be used as a defence against predators, the spurs are believed to be used against other males. No one has died in Australia from platypus venom, but if you're unlucky enough to be a victim, I'm told that even strong drugs like morphine don't stop the enormous pain.

The platypus tail stores fat, which helps it to survive if food is scarce. The future survival of the platypus is directly related to the quality of our waterways and the effect that pollution is having on them, so do your bit to keep them safe.

FRILL-NECKED LIZARD

With its own in-built umbrella, the frill-necked lizard or (frilled lizard) fascinates people in many countries around the world, and here at home, it is the reptile emblem of Australia. The frill-necked lizard has paper-thin folds around its neck, which extend to form the frill; this can be the size of a dinner plate. The frill normally lies down along the animal's back, although when it is annoyed, the frill rises in a circle around its throat supported by the muscles of the tongue and jaws. When the mouth gapes widely, the frill is extended, ruff-like around the head. Among its prey are beetles, termites, caterpillars, ants and other insects.

This lizard sure knows how to protect itself from predators. It first tries to camouflage itself. (Who wants trouble if you can stay away from it?) When threatened, it opens its mouth widely, erecting its frill in a blaze of colour. It's all bluff at this stage, and a few hisses here and there are added to the game plan. It also hops about, fiercely lashing its tail. If these scare tactics don't do the trick, the lizard may decide to climb the nearest tree until it is out of reach. But if forced to stand its ground, the frill-necked lizard can inflict a painful bite with its large canine teeth.

The frill-necked lizard is cold-blooded and uses the environment to maintain the right body temperature. If its body temperature needs to be raised it turns a dark colour, which absorbs heat. As its temperature increases, it becomes a lighter colour.

After mating, in November and December, females lay two or possibly three clutches of 7 to 15 eggs. Hatchlings rely on camouflage for protection against predators, as the frill is initially small and not much use as a bluff.

PERENTIE

To me, the perentie is the king of all lizards! It's the largest lizard in Australia and the second largest lizard in the world. (The Komodo dragon, found in Indonesia, is the largest.) The perentie thrives on the rocky ridges and sandy country of Central Australia. I love the way they proudly roam around, then stand on their back legs to survey their surroundings. At about 2 metres or more standing up, they look pretty imposing.

Perenties can run very fast. I've seen them take off, either on all fours or on their hind legs and by jingles, they're quick! They eat a variety of different animals including lizards, snakes, mammals (even small kangaroos) and birds. They love a challenge and sometimes use their powerful forelegs to dig out prey from a burrow or shelter. They also eat the eggs of birds and reptiles, as well as carrion. Perenties sometimes leave a favourite rock crevice or burrow and take off on an excursion over the surrounding plains, often for several days. They are very patient, and will often just sit and wait for an ideal opportunity to pounce, particularly when they are hunting larger prey.

The perentie is said to be aggressive, and it certainly can be when provoked. As it distends air from its large neck pouch, a fierce hiss comes out warning off attackers. The powerful tail can lash out and deliver a whip-like blow—fast and painful, like the blink of an eye. As a last resort, the perentie may lunge towards its attacker with its mouth open, hissing before quickly retreating to the nearest tree or place of safety.

Mating normally occurs in spring. To keep her eggs away from other predators (like foxes) the female does some excavation work. Around January she lays between six and 11 eggs into a long hole dug underneath a rock and then totally covers it. Young perenties are much more brightly coloured than their parents who are dark brown-black with yellow spots.

DID YOU KNOW ... I know a bloke who saw a perentie run up the back of an Aboriginal hunter and stand on his head after being frightened by a poor spear throw. The perentie must have thought the hunter was a tree! Wouldn't that have been a funny sight?

WOMBAT

With its rounded body and short powerful legs, the wombat is like a little bulldozer! It loves nothing better than to dive head first into a mound of dirt and start burrowing. It digs with its front legs, pushing the dirt out with its hind feet. A wombat's burrow can be up to 20 metres long and can have many separate branch tunnels, allowing for more than one sleeping place. Wombats love to curl up and have a snooze safe underneath the earth in their own little chamber. Mothers share their swag with their young, but otherwise wombats like to stretch out by themselves. A bit like myself.

Burrowing can cause untold damage to fences, because they leave holes large enough for less desirable intruders such as dingoes and rabbits. Their extensive burrow systems, often extending 20 or 30 metres underground, can also destroy valuable pasture.

Australia has three types of wombat: the common, northern hairy nosed and southern hairy nosed. The northern hairy nosed wombat is listed as endangered. The southern hairy nosed wombat does not need to drink and survives by a very low metabolism.

The wombat is found in various habitats in southeastern Australia. It is the largest burrowing herbivore in the world and feeds mainly at night. Because they are not good at regulating their body temperature, wombats wait until the temperature outside the burrow is roughly the same as it is inside before venturing out. Native grasses and roots can be tough to chew, but the wombat's teeth are designed to help it get as much fibre from its food as possible. They certainly get maximum nourishment, because food can take as long as two or three days to pass through the digestive system.

Wombats breed from April to June and about four weeks after mating the baby wombat crawls into the mother's pouch, latching on to her teat. It remains in the pouch for about eight months; then it is strong enough to dig around the burrow. The baby remains with the mother for another 12 months before it goes off on its own. Baby wombats have been likened to puppies, as they love to jump up on their mother and wrestle and play with her.

The common wombat, like all Australian native animals, is a protected species.

KOALA

With their rounded bodies and fluffy ears, koalas are among our most appealing native animals. They are true Australians—fossil remains of koala-like animals have been found that are estimated to be 25 million years old!

Koalas are marsupials—mammals that rear their young in a pouch. Like most marsupials, they are nocturnal. They spend their days slumbering in the forks of eucalypt trees and awaken at dusk. Unlike humans, who sleep roughly eight hours at a time, koalas are lazybones and sleep up to 16 hours a day to conserve energy. Early European settlers thought they were stupid because of these sleeping habits.

If you want to find a koala, you will have to go to the eucalyptus forests of eastern Australia. Koalas are extremely selective about what they will eat, preferring only a few types of eucalyptus species, although they occasionally eat from other trees including wattle, tea tree or paperbark. They eat up to 500 grams of leaves per day. Eucalyptus leaves contain approximately 50 per cent water, so koalas don't often need to drink. I bet you didn't know that the name 'koala' is said to come from an Aboriginal word meaning 'no drink'.

Koalas are very territorial. A male marks his territory by rubbing his chest against the bark of a tree. This causes a secretion from the brown 'scent gland' in the centre of the chest.

Koala mums raise one cub at a time; the young drinks its mother's milk and stays in her pouch for about five months. When it is born, a koala cub is blind.

The koala is a protected animal, although it is not officially classified as endangered. Urban and agricultural development and logging have greatly reduced the koala's natural habitat. In fact, since European settlement, approximately 80 per cent of the koala's habitat has been destroyed.

DID YOU KNOW ... Eucalyptus leaves are poisonous to most animals. Koalas have specific intestinal adaptations which help detoxify leaves. It is a myth that these toxins make the koala 'drunk'.

CHAPTER 3

BIRDS
OF THE OUTBACK

Australia is home to approximately 850 species of birds, ranging from the giant, flightless cassowary to the colourful parrots that inhabit the dry, arid centre. As well as our native birds, we also have many migrant and introduced species. Birds in Australia are found in an extraordinarily wide variety of habitats— from the dry, arid desert, to the rainforests of the tropical north, to the forested woodlands and grassy plains of the east coast.

Australia has many birds that are not found anywhere else in the world. Some of the more well known birds include the kookaburra, the wedge-tailed eagle and the emu. Since European settlement, many birdscapes have changed due to urban development and agriculture and unfortunately, this has resulted in a decline in the numbers of some species.

Our feathered friends grace the sky and their aeronautical abilities have provided inspiration to man since the dawn of time.

This chapter looks at just a few of our amazing birds. Each has its own individual characteristics. Some are born performers who love to sing, some are sneaky even though they can't fly, and some are so obsessed with their tummies that they will let you hand feed them. I hope you love these birds as much as I do!

Egrets prefer to live near streams, rivers and swamps, where food is plentiful. I think they're very elegant.

WEDGE-TAILED EAGLE

What a magical creature the wedge-tailed eagle is. My favourite for sure. When I was a child, I studied them for hours, in awe of their size and ability. The wedge-tailed eagle has a wing-span of up to 2.5 metres and is Australia's largest raptor. The word 'raptor' comes from from the Latin *raptare*, meaning 'to seize and carry off'. This means they are carnivorous birds with sharp beaks and claws for holding their prey and tearing food. Wedgies hunt at sunrise and sunset. They eat mainly rabbits, reptiles, marsupials and carrion, although they have been known to take prey as large as kangaroos.

This eagle can be found in all states of Australia, frequenting a variety of habitats from wooded mountain slopes to treeless plains. There are lots of them near my house.

Wedge-tailed eagles are spectacular fliers. They use their long wings, with six clear feathers at each tip, to soar to heights of up to 2,000 metres or more, riding thermal currents and using their wedge-shaped tail to maneouvre. I have soared the skies with them in my family's *Cessna* aeroplane on many occasions, and even though the plane was ten times their size they still look at me as if to say 'Who do you think you are invading my territory?'. They play cat and mouse with me for a while then dive away into a spiral that only a bird could possibly do.

Like many birds, wedge-tailed eagles mate for life. Breeding usually occurs in July and August. Nests are built high on the top of branches or ledges, giving them a good view of surrounding land. The female lays two eggs, and both parents incubate the eggs for 45 days. Young wedge-tailed eagles are a pale sandy brown; adult males and females have black plumage and a dark brown nape.

A wedgie Mum!
Both wedge-tailed eagles and white-bellied sea eagles line their nests with leaves and sticks. Their nests can be more than 2 metres across.

WHITE-BELLIED SEA-EAGLE

One of the things I love to do is to fly my helicopter along the coastal fringes of the Top End, admiring the magnificent white-bellied sea-eagles, perched high up on a rock or in their nests atop high trees, or sometimes soaring above shallow water in search of a fish for supper. The white-bellied sea-eagle is my second favourite eagle. It is a large white bird of prey with broad greyish wings and a short pale wedge-shaped tail. Not only does it live around Australia's coasts, but also along inland rivers, lagoons, lakes and reservoirs. The white-bellied sea-eagle can be a very noisy bird, especially early morning and evening. It sounds a bit like a goose.

Birds form pairs for life and lay two or occasionally three eggs. Incubation is carried out mainly by the female, with occasional relief by the male. The female tends the young for 65–70 days until fledging takes place, and it is not unusual for two young to be successfully reared. They usually leave their supportive mum and dad about six months after this, finding out what a big and scary world it can sometimes be.

White-bellied sea-eagles are carnivores and feed on scavenged food of birds, mammals, fish, reptiles and carrion. Pairs will often hunt together and they are known to harass other bird species to either steal prey or have them regurgitate it. Their main food is fish as I have often seen, sometimes dead, but mostly caught live. Live fish and sea snakes account for 90–95 per cent of their diet.

The white-bellied sea-eagle has magnified vision, and has visual acuity around eight times that of humans. So large are the eyes that this raptor is unable to move the eye within its socket. It has to rely on head movements to build up a three dimensional picture of its world.

EMU

This imposing creature is Australia's largest bird and the world's second tallest bird after the ostrich. The wings hidden beneath its feathers are not meant for flight, and the emu is happy wandering about wherever its long legs take it. It lives a mostly nomadic lifestyle, travelling in small groups. Emus inhabit much of mainland Australia (including our place Amburla), except rainforest and very arid desert.

Emus feed on young green shoots, insects, fruit and seeds—whatever is available. I've seen them eating out of rubbish bins, even trying out a plastic bag! They also swallow gravelly stones to help grind up food in their gizzards. They are very curious about what is happening around them and are always ready to peck at and pull at anything! Emus are a brownish colour, with a dark-grey head and neck. Their strong three-toed legs can carry them up to speeds of 50 kilometres per hour.

In late summer, the female lays between five and eleven eggs. The male then stays at home sitting on the eggs for an incredible eight weeks. He doesn't eat at all during this time, relying on a layer of fat he has built up for this very task. He rears the brood and stays with them for up to 18 months. He watches for lizards, which eat emu eggs. Chicks are also preyed upon by dingoes, eagles, foxes and feral cats.

Once I caught a young emu on our property. When I picked it up, it pooped all over me (£!^£!*&!)! Its Dad was close by crying out for it. So I pointed it in the Dad's direction, let it go and enjoyed watching them bond again.

These days, emus are farmed for their distinctive meat, which is eaten in some of the world's best restaurants, and emu leather products, including belts, wallets and bags, are also popular. Emu oil was first used as a traditional medicine by Aboriginal tribes. One of its therapeutic benefits is the temporary easing of joint pain. Emu oil is now used in a range of products such as soap, moisturiser, massage oils and shampoos.

KOOKABURRA

With its amused chuckle, the laughing kookaburra has a unique way of introducing itself and is widely recognised all across Australia as a true Outback friend, always there to keep you in good spirits! The kookaburra is also one of the few native birds that has successfully adapted to city and suburban development since European settlement.

Found mainly throughout eastern Australia and the southwest of Western Australia, this famous icon of Australia has been called various colloquial names from the 'laughing jackass' to the 'bushman's clock', this last for providing a great natural alarm clock. A bit like a rooster, I suppose. You don't come across kookaburras in Central Australia, but in the Top End, they keep the place alive. It seems as if they laugh at the people they come across, maybe even acting as our conscience should we do anything silly.

Each family of kookaburras has its own defined territory, and kookaburras generally will use their same nesting site year after year. Kookaburras are very family oriented, and each new chick stays in the family group, forming an extended family network that helps raise the next season's chicks.

The laughing kookaburra is a kingfisher, yet it rarely catches fish, preferring snakes, rodents, lizards and insects. It is known for its patience and will perch high up on telephone poles or trees waiting for some unsuspecting prey. With the help of a bony ridge attached to the back of the skull, the kookaburra will shake its head and bash its prey until it is dead.

Kookaburras are quite cheeky creatures and appear to be mostly unafraid of humans. They have been known to raid picnic areas for tidbits and are able to be hand fed in many areas of Australia.

DID YOU KNOW … Baby kookaburras can't laugh automatically and have to be taught by other family members. Laughter plays a very important role in developing family bonds but is also used to mark territory.

MAGPIE

The magpie is a bossy bird. You'd be hard pressed to go anywhere in Australia and not see one of these birds as it flies about on its day's business. Magpies are among Australia's most common birds. They even have a football team named after them! It is widely recognised by its unique carolling which can be heard from the middle of Australia to urban backyards.

The magpie is related to the currawong and butcherbird family. There are three types of magpie in Australia: the black back, white back and the western. Males and females have similar colouring with a bold white patch on the nape common to all three types.

Magpies feed mainly on ground-dwelling worms and invertebrates, and seeds. They are stickybeaks too, and can often be seen probing into crevices and listening with their heads to one side, trying to locate grubs under the soil by the noise they make as they burrow.

Magpies breed from July to March. The female makes the nest out of sticks, wire, string and plastic—whatever she can find—and lines it with soft material and grass. She lays between three and five eggs, which hatch in 20 days. She rears the young while the male fiercely defends the nest and territory by dive bombing any perceived threat. You don't want to mess with this little terror, as a magpie will strike your scalp and even draw blood should you invade its privacy! Both parents get into flight training for their young and sometimes push against young ones in the air, directing their flight and helping them achieve independence.

Magpies live in a hierarchy with one dominant male, two to three females and up to about 20 young individuals. Magpies normally occupy an area up to 20 hectares depending on the amount of grazing area and trees.

TROY'S TIP

To avoid being attacked by a swooping magpie when you're out walking or cycling, draw a big pair of eyes on the back of your bike helmet; or you can raise one arm high over your head, then let your hand drop in imitation of a swan. The magpie thinks this is a huge eagle or other raptor and often backs off.

PELICAN

The Australian pelican is our largest flying bird. It is easily recognisable with its pink bill, suspended pouch and its slightly prehistoric, sort of pterodactyl look. My young nephew Trent knows all about dinosaurs and the whole prehistoric world. If I want to know anything about them, all I do is ask my little mate Trent.

Pelicans occur throughout the mainland, wherever there is water, but they tend to breed mainly on the south and west coasts and the interior salt lakes. Their nomadic lifestyle and fluctuations in population are often related to water availability. These big birds seem to be always thinking of their tummies and are good at making friends with humans in the hope of receiving a tasty snack. In many areas they have become quite tame and are able to be hand fed.

Despite their size pelicans are great fliers. Their landing is most impressive. They glide along the surface of the water and use their webbed feet as brakes, coming to a skidding stop very much like a plane coming into land.

Both parents look after their chicks. They become experts at wrestling food from a parent's gullet. It makes a funny sight, as the chicks dive into the parent's pouch rummaging for food. All you see is a little pair of webbed feet sticking out of the pouch. Once mobile, the chicks go into day care, in creches of about 30 birds. This protects them from predators and they remain in these groups until they are able to fly, at about three months old.

DID YOU KNOW ... There are fossils of pelican-type birds dating back 30–40 million years.

WILLIE WAGTAIL

This wagtail must be feeling a bit tired, as he's decided to hitch a ride!

These are really cheeky little characters, and yet I reckon us blokes could learn a trick or two from them. Girls love romance and they love to be sung to. The willie wagtail keeps this in mind and sure knows how to court a girl properly. He's a very romantic figure, often found serenading the moon with his sweet song.

Most of us, however, would have seen willie wagtails in the daytime, wagging their tails from side to side or flying in low zigzags as they hop about feeding on insects. The wagtail belongs to a group of birds called fantails. Fantails are so called because they constantly fan their tails as they tumble and twist through the air. Willie wagtails are very resourceful, and are often seen perched on the backs of cattle ready to gobble up any insects the animal may have disturbed in its movements.

DID YOU KNOW ... Wagtails will often re-use nests from previous years by dismantling it and recycling the material. It's good to see them being environmentally friendly, don't you think?

At nesting time, the wagtail is incredibly busy, creatively weaving its nest from grass, bark, cobwebs, and hair from various animals. I've watched them pulling hair from horses' manes and tails, to use in their nests. If its eggs are threatened, the wagtail widens its white eyebrow to signal aggression. Wagtails also swoop at, and chase away dogs, cats, other birds, and even cows. No doubt about it, they are cocky. In fact, they're not scared of anything. Ever heard of the expression 'make a willie wagtail fight a wedge-tailed eagle'? Well, should a wedgie come near its nest, it will have a go at it, be sure of that! However the adults are not always successful in defending their nests; feral cats in particular are a menace, as they are with so much of our native fauna.

BUDGERIGAR

The budgerigar is Australia's most common parrot, and is now internationally popular as a cage bird because of its ability to talk and play games if trained. Budgerigars will perch on top of all sorts of things hoping to bend your ear for a chat. John Gould discovered them in 1794 and since then there have been many different types of budgerigars bred all over the world. The name 'budgerigar' comes from an Aboriginal language and means 'good food'. Aboriginal people considered roasted young chicks a delicacy.

Because of its survival skills and its amazing breeding ability, the budgerigar is probably one of Australia's most abundant birds. It is highly mobile and congregates in large flocks throughout mainland Australia, except for the Top End and coastal areas. You'll find them in lightly wooded scrubland where there is water nearby. There are lots around our desert bores at home—sometimes the blue outback sky looks like a blanket of green carpet has been dragged across it. I love their airborne antics and can sit and watch them for hours, especially around dusk, as they circle the water holes making sure the coast is clear to drop in for a drink.

Budgerigars in the wild don't do much in the way of preparing nests. Their nests are made in the cavities of soft rotting wood with no nesting material—so there's no cleaning up their rooms! The female lays approximately five eggs, and chicks become pretty much independent at about five weeks old.

Although multitudes of birds are destroyed each year by bush fires, heat waves, droughts and storms, the wild budgerigar is in no danger of becoming rare, and it should always continue to be known throughout the world—just as the emu and kangaroo—as a true Australian.

DID YOU KNOW ... During periods of high temperature, budgies remain inert to conserve body moisture. They can survive up to 30 days without drinking.

MAJOR MITCHELL COCKATOO

TROY'S TIP

The Major Mitchell has always been a popular bird in Australian aviculture (rearing birds), but illegal trapping means its numbers fluctuate in the black market cage bird trade. If you want to purchase one of these beautiful birds make sure it is from a reputable breeder.

With its head dress of yellow and red, the magnificent Major Mitchell cockatoo is one of the most colourful characters of the outback. These cheeky birds are my favourite cockatoos.

Named after Sir Thomas Mitchell, who discovered them, these cockatoos are now protected. Sadly, their distribution has diminished in some areas since European settlement. Unlike other cockatoos, Major Mitchells do not hang out in big groups, preferring pairs or small groups. They are found mainly in the arid interior of mainland Australia where water and large nesting trees are available. We have quite a few of them nesting in the trees on our property. They always screech a welcoming g'day as you go past them. Another reason they live in central Australia is that there are lots of wild paddy melons out there. That's their favourite food. They also eat seeds, berries, roots, nuts and fruits and they spend much of their time on the ground foraging.

Breeding takes place from July to January, usually in a hollow limb or tree cavity. The courtship display between the male and female is quite spectacular. The male approaches the female with the body and crest erect, and flicks his head from side to side, uttering an excited call. A bit like musical theatre—singing and dancing all at once. The female lays between one and three eggs, which incubate in 26 days. Fledging usually occurs at about 56 days.

Major Mitchells form strong pair bonds. They enjoy each other's company and they're also are a bit vain and love to preen each other!

SULPHUR-CRESTED COCKATOO

These cheeky cockatoos have plenty of charm, but their singing leaves a lot to be desired! They are gregarious birds with a distinctive yellow crest and are known for their trademark, raucous, harsh screeching. They're not the type of birds you want living close to your house if you want to have a sleep-in in the morning, let me tell you.

Sulphur-crested cockatoos flock at communal roosts for choir practice, employing their screeches with abandon. This makes for a spectacular and noisy display. They forage for berries, seeds, nuts, bulbs and insects, and can at times cause farmers heartache by causing damage to cereal crops. Breeding occurs mainly from August to January; nests are made in tree cavities by both parents chewing around the entrance and inside the hollow (a rather unique way to decorate the house). Tall, dead eucalyptus trees close to or bordering watercourses are preferred nesting sites. I call these trees 'dead dog trees' because they have no bark left on them. Ha!

The clutch normally consists of one to three eggs, which hatch in 30 days. The young chicks fledge at about 70 days, but remain with the parents for an indefinite period of time.

TROY'S TIP

When you see cockatoos foraging on the ground, look up! High in the trees are other cockatoos on guard duty, ready to warn the flock of danger.

CASSOWARY

With a 'helmet' on top of its head, the cassowary looks like it's dressed for a game of rugby. The helmet or 'casque' helps it cut through the underbrush of the forest floor. It also has two distinct pieces of swinging red flesh hanging from its neck. These are called wattles.

Found in the extreme northeast of Australia in dense rainforests, it feeds almost exclusively on fruit fallen from trees onto the rainforest floor. The cassowary plays an important role in spreading rainforest seeds, eating fruit whole and secreting seeds undamaged. They also eat small dead marsupials, insects, frogs and birds.

I'm not sure how well this works though, because a female may breed with several males in a season, deserting each after the eggs are laid! The male incubates the egss and cares for the chicks until they are about nine months old. Good old Dad, no doubt about him!

CHAPTER 4

DANGEROUS CRITTERS

REDBACK SPIDER

There was a redback on the toilet seat when I went there last night. I didn't see him in the dark, but boy, I felt his bite.

A few classic lines from an old Australian singing legend Slim Newton. I can't say for certain, but I bet these words came from a true story, as redback spiders are known to make their homes in many of the classic old outdoor Australian toilets, or dunnies.

Redback spiders are found all over outback Australia, and also in cities. The one you have to look out for is the female as she is the venomous one. She has a large red stripe down her back that she proudly displays—a subtle warning from nature that she is every bit as dangerous as she looks.

Hundreds of people in Australia are bitten each year by the redback. The bite makes them very sick, and many go to hospital to be treated with antivenom. The symptoms of redback bite are a deep pain and localised swelling, followed by nausea, headache, cramp, and in severe cases, paralysis and even death. There have, however, been no deaths from redback bites since 1956, when an effective antivenom was developed.

The web of the redback is easily recognisable because it is very untidy. It is usually spun in damp, dark places (even in empty soft drink cans). This spider spends most of her time in the darkest corner of her web and only comes out if an insect is caught in her trap. That's her dinner.

The female redback is approximately 10 millimetres long and will not normally bite you, unless she is protecting her white egg sacs, or if she comes into contact with your skin. The male is only 4 millimetres long. He has a white tummy and four black stripes down the side of his body.

The female spins up to eight round balls of web around her eggs to protect them. Some of these balls can contain as many as 300 eggs and in warm weather the spiderlings will hatch after about two weeks. Each young spider moults (sheds its skin) several times before reaching its full size, yet only a few reach maturity as, like some other spider species, young redbacks eat each other!

TROY'S TIP

If you see one of these spiders, don't play with it or scratch its tummy, because you may find yourself saying hello to the doctor with a large needle. (I'm a sook when it comes to needles. I hate them, so you won't find me picking them up.)

DID YOU KNOW ... The silk spun by the redback is very strong and was once used for the cross-hairs in the sights of a gun.

SCORPION

Scorpions are one of nature's survivors—they've inhabited the earth for over 400 million years! When I was growing up, I'd see these deadly little soldiers come out from hiding and go on the warpath. This happens in arid Australia when it rains (which is not often—only 250 millimetres a year). Once again, my suggestion is don't mess with them. If you get stung, it can make you very sick indeed!

There are a number of scorpions throughout Australia ranging from smaller ones found in suburban backyards to the largest ones found in the Flinders Ranges in South Australia. The most common and widespread type is the marbled scorpion, which is only about 25 millimetres long.

Scorpions are related to spiders and like them, have a two-part abdomen. The sting is carried in the hind section. Australian scorpions are not a huge danger to humans. Its sting can be painful, but it will wear off if you apply ice to numb the swelling.

With four pairs of walking legs the scorpion can sure rock and roll. On its head is a pair of pincers, which enables it to handle food. The scorpion hides under stones during the day and hunts its prey by night.

There have been only two deaths by scorpions in Australia. Both victims were babies.

CENTIPEDE

It's lucky the centipede doesn't have to wear shoes because most species possess between 21–23 pairs of legs and that's a lot of shoe laces to tie! Speaking of shoes, I remember a story Mum told me. It goes like this—Dad used to be a butcher so he used to start work at around 5 o'clock in the morning. One particular morning he reached down from his bedside in the darkness and slipped on his big butcher boots … ack … Dad let out a yell and hopped around the room while he pulled the boot off. His big toe swelled to twice its normal size—the result of a centipede bite! Dad always tapped his boots upside down from that day on.

A centipede preys on animals much larger than itself, like frogs and mice. Underneath its head it has a pair of fangs used to inject venom into its prey. These fangs are vital, as its jaws are weak. The house centipede is often nicknamed Johnny Hairy Legs; unlike other species, it only has 15 pairs of legs.

Centipedes are found throughout Australia, especially in backyards. Bites may be painful, but there have been no fatalities recorded in Australia. This is because the bites rarely penetrate human skin.

Millipedes are close relations of centipedes. They might be nasty to us, but remember that they're someone else's dinner!

FRESHWATER CROCODILE

The freshwater crocodile, also called the Johnston's crocodile, is found in the river systems and flood plains of northern Australia. It is quite shy, preferring to make its home away from humans. The freshwater crocodile is generally not regarded as being dangerous to humans, but I don't recommend approaching one, as it will retaliate if cornered with a swift attack with its sharp teeth. And let me tell you they are sharp!

The major feature distinguishing the freshwater crocodile from the saltwater crocodile is the shape of its snout. Freshwaters have a longer, narrower snout and are smaller than their saltwater cousins, only averaging 1.2 metres in length. Freshwater crocs can only live in fresh or slightly salty water while the saltwater crocodile can survive in both types of water.

Signs like this are a pretty common sight in crocodile-infested regions of northern Australia.

Like saltwater crocodiles, freshwater crocs kick back in the sun during the day. They spread themselves out in the sand, nice and lazy, with their bellies slung low on the ground. They feed on a diet of fish, crustaceans, tortoises and small vertebrates caught near the water's edge.

Unlike the saltwater crocodile, the freshwater croc breeds during the dry season. The female builds a nesting hole in the sand on the bank of a river, about 10 metres from the water's edge and lays about 20 eggs. The eggs hatch in November and the offspring are guarded by their mother for a short time after hatching. They then join their mother in the water.

The freshwater crocodile has not faced the same persecution as the saltwater crocodile, because its skin is not as valued.

DID YOU KNOW ... A crocodile has a bigger brain than other lizards, but it is still only the size of a match box. You have a bigger brain, so you'll be able to work out that you should stay clear of them. I would if I were you!

SALTWATER CROCODILE

I think of the saltwater crocodile as a prehistoric submarine. This amazing reptile has outlived the dinosaurs! It has no predators except man. It is the largest reptile on earth and can grow up to 8 metres long. The saltwater crocodile is found on Australia's northern tropical coastline, with the largest numbers in the Northern Territory, my backyard.

These crocodiles (also known as estuarine crocodiles) are mainly found in estuaries where tidal rivers meet the sea. But they are also found in swamps, lakes, rivers and even inland in salt or fresh water, dispelling the myth that they are only at home in salt water.

The saltwater crocodile has a strong, muscular body. It is feared by all creatures, because it sneaks up on its prey with only its eyes and nostrils visible. Shallow breathing maintains the right degree of buoyancy, enabling the crocodile to float while remaining hidden from its unsuspecting prey.

The saltwater croc then springs a swift attack, ambushing its prey with the help of its tail. Prey is normally drowned and dismembered. This is where the term 'death roll' comes from. The muscles on its jaw are very powerful; combined with its teeth, the grip is incredibly firm. Interestingly, the teeth are unable to chew and are only used to crush and dismember the catch.

The saltwater crocodile eats crustaceans such as mud crabs, fish and other reptiles such as turtles, birds and mammals. In some cases they attack kangaroos, cattle and horse and store the catch underwater to eat later. Yet for such large animals, they really eat very little and only about once a week.

Their colour varies from grey to dark brown and I have seen a big crocodile close to black. Some Aboriginal friends have told me they've seen a big black crocodile with sand covering its back. This made it look like an island. The funny thing was it had a lily flower growing in the sand on its back!

In the breeding season, which occurs in the flooded wetlands during the wet season from November to April, the saltwater crocodile is quite aggressive. Dominant males may injure or kill other males; dominant females attack other

TROY'S TIP

Stay clear of the water's edge! A crocodile is not your friend. Quite the opposite—it will not hesitate to kill you.

females. The female makes a nest of reeds high up on the bank and digs a hole in the centre where she lays between 50–60 eggs. She guards her nest throughout incubation. Hatchlings are carried to the water and are taught how to swim.

Infant crocodiles are prey for raptors (especially white-bellied sea eagles) and other reptiles, and fewer than 1 per cent of eggs laid result in mature crocodiles.

In the past, crocodiles were aggressively hunted for their skin, and scientists believed they were close to extinction. I have flown my helicopter extensively throughout northern Australia and I don't believe they were in danger of extinction. Hunters did have an impact in some accessible areas, but northern Australia covers thousands of kilometres of inhospitable waterways, some impossible to get to by road or bush track. In fact, government experts would do well to listen to experienced bush people when it comes to controlling crocodile numbers.

For instance, many large crocodiles have been taken from their territorial waters to protect tourists and fishermen, but this has backfired. Old man crocs always protect their hunting areas and don't allow young crocs to come past their marked territory. With their removal, hundreds of young saltwater crocodiles have made their way up the rivers and are increasing in numbers. What does this mean? Young crocs become old man crocs, and with more of them in the rivers, the danger to tourists and fishermen has increased.

Have you heard the phrase 'crying crocodile tears'? It means that the person doing the crying is perhaps not genuinely upset and is trying to gain sympathy. So do crocodiles actually cry? As a matter of fact they do, but it's not an emotional response. Like human tears, they are products of glands that produce a fluid to help clean and protect the eye. Tears are normally only visible if the crocodile has been out of the water for a long time and the eyes are in danger of drying out.

During the day the saltwater crocodile basks in the sun. As its body heats up, it lies with its head towards the sun, its mouth open to reduce the effect of heat on its brain. When temperatures are high, it returns to the water, seeks shade, or coats its body with mud. Keeping the mouth open is called thermo-regulating (maintaining a body temperature between 30° and 32°C).

DID YOU KNOW ...
If the temperature is about 32°C, then the young will be male. If it is below 31°C or above 33°C, then the young are more likely to be female.

CHAPTER 5

SPECIAL SPOTS

Australia is a land of great beauty, there's no question about that! Our landscapes are among the oldest and most spectacular on the planet. I travel around the country a lot and I am constantly overwhelmed by the beauty found in every state and territory. There are many spots that are special to me, and this chapter looks at only a few. These are in my home state of the Northern Territory, to me the best place on earth!

The centre of Australia is also associated with the creation stories of the Aboriginal Dreamtime. Aboriginal people have had a long and happy relationship with the land and it's only in recent years that the rest of us have begun to truly appreciate their care of the land and their kinship with it—the land forms a crucial part of the Aboriginal spirit. When you come across a sacred site, it's easy to feel the sense of awe experienced by our indigenous brothers and sisters. Remember, though, that these places have deep spiritual significance to Aboriginal people and we should respect them.

It's no surprise that the Australian outback is a great attraction to tourists, from all around the country and from many countries around the world. I'm proud that our land is a favoured destination for people from as far away as Europe, Russia, Asia, the Americas and Africa. In fact, tourism is one of the biggest industries in the Territory. Now people everywhere are beginning to see the grandeur, the mystery and the vibrant colours of central Australia.

Rainbow Valley would have to be one of the prettiest spots in the outback, bar none. When I walk through it, I feel hungry because the colours remind me of neopolitan ice cream—from chocolate to vanilla to strawberry. And the colours change dramatically all the time, especially when we've had a bit of rain around, and mirages and reflections off the pools give you hundreds more perspectives. When water is reflected, it shows off the valley in a very proud way. I love it here.

ULURU (AYERS ROCK)

Two-thirds of this amazing rock is still in the ground. My latest memory of the place was with my friends at the local Aboriginal community. We played a bit of country music with my Uncle Scottie around the base of the rock—and had a contest for the best outback rapper. I learned a lot about the Dreamtime during that time with the family. There is so much to learn about the sacred sites surrounding the rock. I climbed it when I was 19, but I don't think I'll climb it again, as the tribal elders have decreed that they do not appreciate people walking all over it.

When it rains it so beautiful. Waterfalls are created and rock holes are full of water. The animals and birds come to drink here, so it's a lifeline for them. When Aboriginal people lived off the land around there, it was a perfect place to get out of the weather and to wait as bush tucker, like kangaroos and wallabies, came in for fresh water. The best way to wrap up a tour of Uluru is to watch the effect the sun moving down over the horizon has on the colours of the western wall of the rock. One of world's truly spectacular sights!

KATA TJUTA (OLGAS)

Some 50 kilometres west of Uluru are the ancient and mysterious Olgas (Kata Tjuta). This place is so completely different from the Rock, the contrast is amazing. Made up of more than fifty weathered domes, the Olgas rise over 600 metres from the surrounding plain where the wind has carved some massive curves. I regard this awesome collection of domes as even more powerful and spectacular than the neighbouring Uluru, especially in spring when the place is amazingly blue.

Some say Mount Olga derives its name from the wife of a Spanish king called Amadeus. The Pitjantjatjara tribe call it Kata Tjuta, meaning 'many heads'. The two principal domes, Ghee and Walpa, are dedicated to Wanambi the Rainbow Serpent. Strong winds can suddenly whip up through the gorges. They say this is caused by the Rainbow Serpent's breath, warning intruders of his presence. Should a rainbow suddenly appear above Walpa Gorge, the intruder had better run, as this is the Rainbow Serpent preparing to steal his spirit!

Kata Tjuta has many stories. I like the one about the Pungalunga Men, giant cannibal gods who arrived from the west at the time of the Dreaming. They hunted Aborigines with 'tjunas' (throwing sticks). The caves in the lower domes are depressions made in the ground by these giants. Another story says that the domes on the western side are transformed Pungalunga Men sitting around their campfires. And in the central valley of the Olgas are scattered boulders inhabited by Minggara Mice Girls, rape victims of the Pungalunga Men. Descendants of the Pungalunga have been seen in recent years. They are Australia's equivalent of the Himalayan Yeti and America's Big Foot. It's just as well that tourists are forbidden to visit the Olgas after dark!

KINGS CANYON

Only 250 kilometres from the Olgas and Uluru is a completely different contrast of countryside again. Kings Canyon is Australia's baby Grand Canyon. This enormous 300 metre canyon, with sheer cliffs all around, is literally teeming with wildlife and birds. I love to fly my helicopter through it. Even from the air I can feel the strong spiritual significance this place has for local Aboriginal people.

Explorer Ernest Giles named it after one of his sponsors, Fielding King, in 1872. About the same time he spotted and named Ayers Rock. He was obviously a bloke who got around the outback well. Of course, white explorers weren't the first to enter these places. There have been Aboriginal people here—the Luritja people—for 20,000 to 30,000 years.

The high red sandstone walls of Kings Canyon guard something very special—the canyon's greenest spot, 'The Garden of Eden'. It's easy to see why it's called this! The constant water supply supports lush growth of ferns, river red gums, cycads and cypress palms. That's the bigger stuff. But all around you, there are smaller shrubs, flowering bushes and native grasses. In fact, the park contains more than 600 plant species—one third of all the plant types found in Central Australia—and 60 of those species aren't found anywhere else but in Watarrka Park. There are so many insect species in the waterholes that the experts are still counting them. You can see why the Luritja people, who are still custodians for the area, tried to chase Giles away when he first turned up.

Kings Canyon is part of the Watarrka National Park. It is one of the most beautiful sites in Central Australia, and is home to native mice, red kangaroos, black-footed wallabies, dingoes and euros. If you visit Kings Canyon give yourself at least 24 hours in order to experience its tranquillity.

FINKE RIVER

This is meant to be the oldest river in Australia, if not the world, following its present course for over 100 million years. When it does flow, that is! It's never very full, but in the last year we have had more rain than in many decades and the Finke was flowing bank to bank again. It also happens to be one of the lifelines for Lake Ayer, along with the many others that come from the Channel Country. The river is beautiful and many white gums run along its banks. It runs close to my home. In fact the river starts in our very own West MacDonnell Ranges. I love flying over the river after rain and seeing all the little creeks running off the rocks and gullies.

RED BANK GORGE

This is part of where the Finke River starts. The amazing colours change every day of the year. It's a special gorge and was home to my close friends, the Mortons, until they gave it to the national park. It is a very peaceful walk inside, and if you're lucky, you'll see a range of animal life there. Red Bank Gorge is in the middle of the Outback and you feel like you're a million miles from anywhere. It's also very adventurous. You can follow the paths up to different parts of the canyon. And to top it off, it's only a day and a half's walk from my home, Amburla.

MOUNT CONNOR

Sturt's desert pea.

In the early days of discovery, many people mistook Mount Conner for Ayers Rock. When I first saw it when I was a kid, I imagined a big line of Native Americans (we called them Indians back then) lined up on top, ready to pounce on the US Cavalry in some Arizona-type landscape. The flat top stands out for miles and miles—it's really a massive landmark. If you ever want a bearing in the landscape as you fly through, you can use Mount Conner as it stands out forever. I always use it as one of my bearings when I'm flying south of Alice Springs. The wildflowers like mustard bush, Sturt's desert peas and wild hops are abundant after a winter rain. It's something everyone should see!

DEVILS MARBLES

Once again a totally different contrast! The Devils Marbles, carved by the wind, are 400 kilometres north of Alice Springs. They are set in a very dry part of Outback Australia where it would seem no wildlife could possibly live. But they are out there, you just need to know where to look. Watch yourself though, because you might come across an angry king brown! The story goes that devils would use these boulders as their marbles. I'm glad they haven't rolled any when I was climbing them!

If you're lucky, you may spot a bearded dragon. They're all over Central Australia.

SIMPSON'S GAP

Simpson's Gap is just out of my home town, Alice Springs, and is a major landmark for tourists. It is still part of the national park of the West MacDonnell Ranges. You can see why I say everyone should discover them some time! Black-footed wallabies and lots of reptiles live near the Gap, and it was around here that they found the endangered bilby, a kind of Australian rabbit. Rangers and scientists have learned a lot about the land around Simpson's Gap, and they will continue to find out more. That's life, you just never stop learning.

PALM VALLEY

Palm trees in the outback? Red rocks and amazing green palms! It is quite staggering to see this in the middle of the desert. The only other place that I have seen it in the outback is up near Mataranka, on the Roper River, some 1,000 kilometres north. These palm trees were probably brought in by the Afghan camel men when they first came through here, opening up the country. Wouldn't you love to have this as your back garden?

MOUNT SONDER

After rain, the Finke River becomes a blue line heading towards Mount Sonder.

This is no doubt one of the loveliest places for me in the outback. It's got to be my favourite mountain. And it's very close to home, only 30 kilometres. Our property is just north of the Range while Mount Sonder sits right in the middle of it. I can fly there in 15 minutes. It's also close to Glen Helen, which the Finke River runs through. I guarantee that if you come out this way you will be well rewarded by this view alone. It's a spectacular landscape, and not only one of my favourite places, but a favourite of many locals.

CHAMBERS PILLAR

Another amazing place used as a landmark for pioneers and explorers since they first started crossing the Simpson Desert is Chambers Pillar. I know my great-uncle, Ted Colson, used it when he crossed it with a mob of camels in 1936. They even have a section near the Pillar called Colson's Point in honour of him, which always makes me feel proud. The area feels as old as time itself. It's awesome to think how this bit of sandstone and siltstone has continued to stand there over hundreds of millions of years as every other bit of the area has weathered away. Again this is all within a crow's fly of Uluru, but such different country. What a wonderful land we live in!

LITCHFIELD PARK

This is one of the best national parks I've seen in the country, especially just after a good wet season when there are some truly gorgeous waterfalls, like Tully Falls, which is quite wonderful after a rain. With so many waterfalls spread out, I believe this western side of the Stuart Highway is even more fascinating than the Kakadu side—especially from a helicopter pilot's point of view. I remember flying my chopper and landing at the foot of one of the waterfalls not far from Tully, off the beaten track away from any roads, and going for a swim with my film crew when we were doing *Outback Adventures*. We were probably among the few white people ever to have swam in this amazingly clear and clean water. But we were not alone ... it was also home to a very mean-looking 3 metre crocodile. We moved on!

The magnificent Tully Falls, part of the beautiful Litchfield National Park.

AMBURLA

This is home for me. We are north of the West MacDonnell Ranges. While most of the MacDonnell Ranges are highly commercial and developed for tourism, our section is relatively untouched and very rich in wildlife. This is because we protect our roos, wallabies, emus and stock. Having flown all over the outback, I would have to say it has some of the strongest colonies of wildlife in Australia. A little piece of paradise. (Always remember, however, that all properties are private and trespassers can be prosecuted.) We want to keep Amburla as natural as possible so it won't be overgrazed and overstocked; it will be kept viable for our Brahman stud. Our Brahmans are now becoming well known in the cattle industry, for their quality and ability to do well in tough conditions. We have brought in some beautiful cattle from the best Queensland Brahman studs in recent years, crossed good stock from American Brahmans and now have twelve years of our own blood lines. We are really proud of this.

Amburla is my sanctuary, my home away, my family. It's such a peaceful place for me, and there's no better place for me to ride my bike or my horse, or fly my chopper around. I always claim if God didn't live in the Northern Territory, He surely would come to our place for holidays.

Below: An aerial view of some of our Brahman cattle. The beautiful Western MacDonnell Ranges are in the background.

Bottom: Sunset at Amburla. Aren't the colours something else!

CHAPTER 6

OUTBACK LEGENDS

Australian history is full of colourful and inspiring tales of the people and animals who have become legends because of the contribution they have made in shaping the character of this great land. Some admittedly, are more infamous than others and are known for their often questionable, sometimes dangerous, rugged ways.

The bushrangers Ben Hall and Ned Kelly ruled the roads and countryside and had very little regard for authority. This gave them heroic status and they have been romanticised as legendary figures. To this day many find this a national mystery. Their tales are full of adventure and excitement and often, harsh struggles. One thing is certain—'Stand and deliver' and 'Such is life', famous words of two of our memorable bushrangers—have gone down in our history and are now part of the national spirit. And who could forget the great cattle duffer (thief), Harry Redford, who undertook a huge journey with stolen cattle over some of Australia's most rugged terrain.

Others, like John Flynn and RM Williams, worked against unbelievable odds. John Flynn's vision delivered a vital health care service to the Outback that at the time was thought impossible. This service continues today. RM Williams will also forever have a place in Australian history as the man who helped outfit the men and women of the land. From a very young age, Sidney Kidman defied great odds to shape a life that was truly inspiring. The term 'travelling on Kidman land' became another popular expression of the times.

Both Banjo Paterson and Mary Durack brought their great love of the Australian bush to us through stories and verse that continue to move and delight people many years later. And let's not forget Australian working dogs. They are very much a part of the Outback!

I hope you enjoy the tales of these fascinating, often larger than life, characters who have all contributed in their own way to making a unique Australia.

A road train is one of the most awesome sights you're likely to see on Outback roads. They transport anything from large numbers of stock to petrol, so they're an absolutely essential part of life in the Outback. They've got to be something of an Outback legend!

BANJO PATERSON

Anyone who knows me knows that Banjo Paterson is my hero. My father is one of my mentors, and if Banjo were alive today, he'd be one too! Banjo's poetry and stories capture the colour and humour that permeated life in rural Australia. In his day, his writing was phenomenally popular; he created enduring myths and poems that are recognisable worldwide. It's a pity his poems are not currently compulsory reading in our primary schools. I think they should be, to help kids learn more about our heritage.

Andrew Barton Paterson was born in 1864, at Narambla, New South Wales. Much of his early life was spent near Yass, where he pursued his two greatest loves—horses, and the fascinating bush characters he later wrote about so vividly. At the age of 16, Banjo became an articled clerk in a Sydney lawyer's office. It was during this time that he began writing for *The Bulletin*. His readers knew him only as 'The Banjo' (named after an ex-racehorse of his father's) and his identity remained unknown to his readers for a decade.

Banjo's work as a lawyer in Sydney was fulfilling, but he disliked city life. It was the solitude and comfort of the bush that he sought during his numerous trips to remote areas in Queensland and the Northern Territory. In 1889, *Clancy of the Overflow* was published, followed a year later by *The Man From Snowy River*. In early 1895, after a trip to far west Queensland, he wrote one of his greatest works, *Waltzing Matilda*. So by the age of 30, he had penned three classic pieces, and his great sense of Australianism provided a valuable contribution to the emerging national consciousness.

In later years, Banjo worked as a journalist, sports reporter, feature writer and broadcaster. He published memoirs of his wartime experiences, and a novel, *The Shearer's Colt*, which reflects his great love of horse-racing. Banjo died in 1941 at the age of 76. He was a great Australian and if I could meet anyone I wanted, Banjo, you and I would be having a yarn over a cup of billy tea in a place we both love—the Australian bush.

[DID YOU KNOW ... When *The Man from Snowy River* was released, it broke all publishing records in Australia.

JOHN FLYNN

John Flynn was an amazing visionary, a man before his time, who achieved an incredible feat. Combining medicine, aviation and radio with his fierce determination and his deep faith in God, John Flynn brought health care to people living in remote areas of Australia. His vision saw a vital service created, one that is still an essential part of outback life today—The Royal Flying Doctor Service.

Imagine the scepticism Flynn faced at a time when the aeroplane was still a wonder and transmitting and receiving sets had not yet been manufactured. His suggestion that a 'flying doctor' could work from an inland base communicating by radio, and bringing patients to a base hospital, was immediately met with opposition. Yet Flynn remained undaunted. The first breakthrough came when Alf Traegar, an electrical engineer, developed a two-way radio set, enabling people from isolated stations to communicate with the flying doctor base. Then, in late 1927, Flynn's dream was realised when the *Victory*, a single-engined aircraft took off on its first flight with a doctor on board. In its first year Dr Vincent Welch and his pilot flew more than 30,000 kilometres and treated over 255 patients. The service now has bases all over Australia providing much needed medical services. John Flynn died in July 1951. In 1956, a church dedicated to his memory was completed in Alice Springs.

Sir Robert Menzies said that the Royal Flying Doctor Service represented the 'greatest single contribution to the effective settlement of the far distant back country that we have witnessed in our time...'.
What a special place in history 'Flynn of the Inland' holds.

John Flynn's ashes were placed in a grave a few kilometres west of Alice Springs—at the very centre of the vast territory that he was so passionate about.

AUSTRALIAN WORKING DOGS

Living on the land you come to rely on a number of things to tame the tough terrain, like motorised machinery, motorbikes, horses, and my favourite, the Australian cattle dog. A bloke couldn't get a better buddy to hang out with than this loyal dog. Working dogs help control herds that graze across the vast bushland. It's rare to find a landowner who won't boast of the intelligence and loyalty of his four-legged mate. It makes for some tall stories around a campfire, let me tell you. The three breeds recognised as working dogs are the blue heeler, the border collie and the kelpie.

CATTLE DOG

The Australian cattle dog is my favourite breed of dog for sure. I know so many people across Australia who have a 'bluey' to help them get through their day on the land. They also make great pets, like my good old mate Oakie who starred in many episodes of *Outback Adventures*. The Australian cattle dog is also known as the Australian heeler, Queensland heeler or blue heeler. 'Heeler' refers to its herding skill of snapping and biting cattle's heels.

When you're chasing bulls, there's no better mate than a blue heeler.

KELPIE

The kelpie is another great breed of working dog. Kelpies have great intelligence and are able to work all day even in extreme heat. They are fast and can manoeuvre very well, both in yards and in open country. Without doubt, the kelpie has contributed to the Australian sheep industry. Kelpies make great pets. My Dad has one called Ajax.

BORDER COLLIE

Border collies originated along the border between Scotland and England for the purpose of herding sheep and cattle. They are excellent working dogs because they are intelligent, have great athletic ability and by instinct are gatherers. They can stare sheep into submission by using their 'eye'. These dogs are happiest when they are working and need to be kept very active. If there are no sheep or cattle for them to herd they may try their hand at rounding up all sorts of things, including chickens and even children!

Top: Devlin is an Australian shepherd and a cousin of the border collie.

Left: Gypsy is a border collie/kelpie cross. Sometimes farmers breed the two to combine the intelligence and athletic ability of both breeds.

Right: Bruce is a red kelpie and is a well known performer!

MARY DURACK

The role of women and their contribution to the making of Australia was considerable. They reared large families, fed, clothed and educated them. They fought not only isolation and loneliness, but became expert at making do and dealing with droughts, floods, plagues, and death. In short, they stood beside their men and helped open up this great land of ours. As they say, behind every successful man is a great woman!

Mary Durack remains a strong shining example of the remarkable contribution women have made to Australia. Born in Adelaide in 1913 she spent her earliest years on cattle stations in the East Kimberley district. After her schooling, Mary wrote about station life. Her sister Elizabeth, a talented illustrator, sketched for her. Mary's stories were later to be published serially in *The Bulletin*. The editor recognised the appeal her warm accounts of station life had for the public.

In 1937 she joined the staff at the West Australian Newspapers where she pursued her love of writing. She married and raised four daughters and two sons. During this time, she wrote numerous books, plays, stories and articles. She also maintained close ties to the Aboriginal people of the Outback in both rural and urban areas, serving on the Aboriginal Cultural Foundation board. It is perhaps her work *Kings in Grass Castles* that she is most famous for. With themes of Australia's great pastoral industry and the rise of the great cattle kings, it is now studied in schools all over Australia. The *Guardian* said of her that she gave 'a first rate contribution to the social history of the outback'.

The Warburton Ranges on a beautiful clear night. Mary Durack loved the Western Australian outback.

RM WILLIAMS

This bloke is a mate of mine and a true gentleman. Reginald Murray Williams is now known everywhere as RM. His earliest recollections are of people around him making things. His father made everything from horseshoes to plough parts, and a hammer on the anvil was music to his ears. In his early teens, he left home in the mid-north of South Australia, to take up work as a lime burner in the mallee scrub of northwestern Victoria. The skills learnt in this work, together with his will to succeed and his sense of adventure, saw him, at 16, heading for the remote gold fields of Western Australia. He worked as a camel boy surveying huge tracts of arid land. He then worked at a number of the huge pastoral stations of Central Australia, where he learned bush lore from local Aboriginal people, the skills of the mounted stockman from the tough bushmen of the cattle camps.

During the Great Depression, Williams set up camp hundreds of kilometres north of Adelaide at Italowe Gorge in the remote Gammon Ranges. Here he began to craft boots, bush saddlery and equipment used on surrounding stations. It wasn't long before his work developed a reputation for craftsmanship and durability. He returned to Adelaide and began selling his riding boots by mail order. Handcrafted, comfortable and made to last a lifetime, they were developed by a man who understood the hardship and dangers of life in the harsh Australian Outback. It's interesting to know that even after RM made his fortune, he returned to live in the bush. This is where he felt truly happy. These days RM Williams's range of clothing and boots are the stuff of legend, and I know they will be worn by people for many generations to come. In fact, his clothing is often called the 'uniform of the Outback'.

Above: Sturdy saddles are a must when you're working all day on your horse. RM knew this!

Left: Working and adventuring in the unforgiving conditions of Central Australia and other parts of the Outback, RM knew how important it was—and is—for people on the land to have the right gear.

DID YOU KNOW ... RM Williams has been declared a Living Legend and an Australian National Treasure.

SIDNEY KIDMAN

The Outback hasn't changed much since Kidman's day, except for road trains shifting cattle longer distances. Cattle herds are still moved across vast tracts of land!

What a dead-set living legend! With five shillings in his pocket, a one-eyed, lame horse and his swag, Sidney Kidman left home at the age of 13 to pursue work that he had heard drovers talk about. Forty years later, we have an extraordinary tale of a man who went on to own more land than any other individual in Australia. Amazingly, at one stage, Kidman owned 3.5 per cent of Australia's land area and it was often said that when you were travelling across Australia, you were on Kidman land.

With the help of £400 from his grandfather's estate, Kidman went into partnership with his brother Sackville and purchased a half share in his first station in Owen Springs, southwest of Alice Springs, only a couple of stations from my home, Amburla. In 1887, he established a coaching business, running coaches throughout New South Wales and Queensland, but during the depression of the 1890s, most of these were sold. Sidney and his brother began buying cattle stations instead. Kidman reasoned that if he purchased a string of stations stretching from South Australia up to the Gulf of Carpentaria, he could keep stock in better condition by moving them on to greener pastures during drought.

Within a few years he and his brother had bought many stations. I reckon that's not bad for a young bloke who left home at 13 with not much more than the clothes on his back. He eventually acquired either full or part ownership of over 100 stations, including the huge Victoria River Downs in the Northern Territory. It is unlikely that we will ever see a single person ever possess as much land as once owned by the amazing 'cattle king'. Mate, I take my hat off to you. A mighty man, one I admire deeply!

ELSIE COLSON

My great-grandmother, Elsie Colson, was just one of many pioneer women who followed their men to various isolated regions in the Outback. The men moved around a bit depending on the availability of jobs, and the women became skilled at picking up, moving on and setting up again in another remote area. Cooking on open fires and living in tents or bark huts were everyday experiences. Women like Elsie endured great hardships, yet they managed to provide their families with wholesome food, and a mother's tender loving care. Without a doubt, these pioneer women really held home and hearth together, making it possible for the menfolk to succeed on the land.

CAPTAIN STARLIGHT

If you visit Longreach, residents will tell you the tale, passed down the generations, of big Harry Redford, known as King of the Cattle Duffers (thieves). Redford became famous when he undertook a 3,200-kilometre journey through some of Australia's toughest unexplored terrain with well over 1,000 head of stolen cattle. He has come to be known as Captain Starlight, a name drawn from Rolfe Boldrewood's Australian classic *Robbery Under Arms*. Boldrewood allegedly based his central character upon a combination of bushrangers and Harry Redford. However, he was apparently unaware of the existence of an actual bushranger called Captain Starlight whose real name was Frank Pearson.

Redford and his mates, so the story goes, mustered 1,000 cattle out of Bowen Downs and travelled along the Barcoo River and Cooper Creek, down the Strezlecki Track into South Australia. They continued on to Blanchwater Station where they sold the entire herd for £5,000. Redford returned to the east, where he faced charges of cattle stealing. Unfortunately for Redford, a big white bull, part of the herd, was recognised. The white bull was shipped to Queensland and was tendered as evidence at his trial. Amazingly, however, the jury returned a verdict of not guilty!

BEN HALL

Ben Hall is said to have begun bushranging for two reasons. The first was the break-up of his marriage (his wife left him for a former policeman). The second was police persecution—early in his career, the police held him in detention for a month, and when he returned home, Ben found that his property had been vandalised and his cattle stolen. Disappointment and disillusionment overtook him, and secured his future in bushranging.

During his career he captured more than twelve police officers, committed ten mail robberies, more than 20 hold-ups on station properties and numerous hold-ups of entire towns. But perhaps his greatest feat was holding up the mail coach from Gundagai to Yass while it was heavily armed. But Ben was always courteous—even when robbing women of their jewellery!

He never killed anyone, although others of his gang did. In fact, the New South Wales government called on Ben Hall, Charlie Gilbert and Johnny Dunn to surrender or be 'outlawed' after the killing of a police sergeant during a robbery. 'Outlaw' status was an extreme measure—outlaws could be shot dead by anyone in the community. The trio was the first in Australia's history to receive this ruling, but Ben promised: 'They'll never hang Ben Hall'.

A week later, on 5 May 1865, he was dead, betrayed by a 'friend', Mike Connelly, who wanted the £2,000 reward. Hall was gunned down by police. It was said that 36 bullets were found in his body. He was 27 years old.

NED KELLY

For some, Ned Kelly was no more than a criminal, but for others he was brave, daring and a bit of a larrikin—someone distinctly Australian. He has been described as 'one of the most romantic figures in Australian history' and as 'the father of our national courage'. The most notorious of Australian bushrangers, Kelly was a gang leader who started his criminal career by stealing horses and cattle.

He was born at Beveridge, Victoria, in 1855. His father died when he was 12 and his family settled near relatives at Greta, 240 kilometres northeast of Melbourne. It was wild, rugged country and life was hard. At the age of 15, Ned was brought before the Police Court on a charge of assault, and with aiding the bushranger Harry Power in some of his robberies. Although found not guilty, he was later sentenced to six months' hard labour for assault and indecent behaviour. In 1878 a police officer called Fitzpatrick accused Ned's mother of attacking him and Ned of shooting him in the wrist. Ned claimed Fitzpatrick brought on the attack by assaulting one of Ned's sisters, but Mrs Kelly was sent to prison for three years and a £100 reward was offered for Ned's capture. From that time on Ned and his brother Dan kept to the bush. Together with Joe Byrne and Steve Hart, they formed what became known as the Kelly gang.

In October 1878, the gang came across police camped at Stringy Bark Creek. Ned called on the officers to surrender, but they resisted, and in the fight which followed, Ned shot them dead. The reward for Kelly and his gang rose to £2000. Later, it rose to £8000, equivalent to around $2 million! But Ned had many supporters and for almost two years they helped the gang dodge police. Ned explained his killing of police at Stringy Bark as self-defence.

In June 1880 Ned made his last stand. A bitter gun battle between the gang and police raged for hours. Three gang members were killed, and Ned, badly wounded, was arrested. But what a tough man. He survived the bullets, only to be sent to Melbourne gaol, where, on 11 November 1880, he was hanged. He was 25 years old.

Glenrowan, site of Ned Kelly's last stand. To the last, his mocking courage never deserted him and to be 'as game as Ned Kelly' came to mean, in Australian folk language, heroism of a reckless, audacious kind.

CHAPTER 7

OUTBACK ARTISTS

By now, you'll have certainly realised how much I love the Australian Outback. Many of us do! I thought it might be nice to have a chapter in this book that included some of the best artists we have in Australia today. Just one look at the paintings in this chapter will be enough to show you how much the stunning landscapes of the bush have inspired the creative juices of these talented artists.

There are quite a few associations of artists around the country and they all have something to offer both artists and people who love art. In fact, checking out some of these associations is a great way to find out where you can view, and even buy, works of artists who appeal to your tastes. The Australian Guild of Realist Artists is made up of highly committed professional artists, and it provides, among other things, a forum where assistance and advice can be found. Some of the artists in this chapter are members of the Guild. And what would outback art be without the great Albert Namatjira? He's one of my all time favourites. You'll find a few words on Namatjira on pages 90–91.

I hope you like the artists included here. It's a wonderful thing to be able to re-create the fabulous Australian landscapes. Maybe some of you might be inspired to take up a paint brush and let your imaginations run wild!

Aboriginal art is, of course, the oldest art we have in this great land, and rock paintings go back many thousands of years. This rock painting of Wandjina is from the Kimberley in Western Australia. A Wandjina is an Aboriginal spirit person and is closely associated with the sky, the rain and the Rainbow Serpent.

BELINDA WILLIAMS

Belinda Williams is a talented watercolourist who has blossomed into one of the most exciting talents in the Australian art world. A passionate love of landscapes and the outback has taken Belinda to Broken Hill, the Kimberley region, Central Australia and her own backyard of Moree in northwestern New South Wales. The Kimberley region, in particular, has become a special place in Belinda's heart. Its isolation, character and rich tapestry of colour draw her back year after year.

Belinda became a full-time artist in 1996, when she realised that her passion to paint had to come first in her life. She has held a number of solo exhibitions and is a member of the newly formed Stockmans Artists of Australia. Her studio is the shearing quarters on the family property, Carossa. It is from here that she captures images of our wonderful country on canvas. Belinda is a very talented friend of mine, and I believe it won't be long before she's a household name in Australia.

'Ormiston Gorge, Northern Territory'. I really love the ghost gum in this painting. It's hard to go beyond the beauty of the bush for artistic inspiration!

CONNELL LEE

The Australia Connell Lee chooses to paint is the Australia of the hills and the plains. His favourite subjects are the river flats and shearing sheds, red gums and corrugated iron. These are some of my favourite images too, that's for sure. It is the landscape of his youth that Connell returns to in his work, saying that even though much has changed, much remains as it always was. It's difficult to describe Connell's love for the bush: as an artist, his interest lies in the visual truth. His hope is that in depicting 'the bush' in all its variety, truthfully and with insight, he will create a record for present and future generations to enjoy.

Connell's work achieved international recognition at an early age, and at home he is recognised as one of the country's leading illustrators having worked for most of Australia's leading book publishers and business corporations. He has designed stamps for Australia Post; and in 1996, he won *Australian Geographic*'s 'best illustrator of the year' award.

'The Shearing Shed.' Connell's painting really captures what it's like when the shearing season begins. It's hard work!

DI KING

'Galahs Galore.' Galahs are found practically all over Australia. With their distinctive pink breast and grey backs, they're pretty hard to miss. And aren't they cheeky!

Born and educated in Victoria, Di started painting in 1980. Di loves depicting charcters of rural and urban life as well as painting landscapes and even cattle drives (which I know a thing or two about). Whether it is a crisp early morning or the cold of the night Di delights in capturing the essence of light, sensitivity and femininity. It's important for her to know her subject before painting, so she likes to be familiar with whatever texture and form her subject takes.

Her favourite time of day is early morning (mine too) especially when it is frosty or dewy. Di's paintings show everyday activities like a stroll through the bush or cattle grazing in a wonderfully realistic light. Di believes (like me) that we have an abundant country with awe-inspiring views and panoramas. Her favourite place is her home state of Victoria where the magnificent Murray river runs. She's an award winning artist with a love of this great land. Keep doing what you love best, Di!

PETER BROWNE

Peter Browne claims to have been found under a sheet of tin in West Wyalong around 1947 but as a self-confessed eccentric we're not sure whether to believe him! Raconteur and scallywag, Peter carved a life for himself in a ruined cottage in Silverton, 1400 kilometres west of Sydney and commenced full-time painting 20 years ago in oils. His style centres on Australian folklore humour and wildlife, particularly emus. Peter says that he gets his inspiration from the people he meets and he gets to know many people at his gallery. Peter's artwork has also been depicted on tourist cars, coaches, and his own beloved Volkswagon. Peter takes a light-hearted approach to everything, including his artwork, and has been known to cut paintings in half for people seeking a discount!

Peter's works are represented in many private collections. His outback studio has been the subject of outback documentaries. He continues to pride himself that he has managed to keep his paintings out of the National Gallery. *The Bulletin* describes him as 'probably the nation's most Australian artist'.

'Emus.' These are amazing birds and a great Australian icon. You can find out more about emus on page 36.

CHRISTINE PORTER

Rural artist Christine Porter has achieved worldwide success with her watercolours and etchings and has over 70 awards to her credit. She is represented extensively in public and private collections, including that of the Brisbane City Council and many regional shire collections. In 1997 she was elected as a member of the exclusive Australian Watercolour Institute and in 1998 was one of only six artists chosen to represent Australia in the Biennial International Watercolour Exhibition in Mexico City.

She has worked as a governess, station cook, teacher and artist, and it was during this time that she concentrated on domestic and agricultural themes. She was especially interested in the way the sun created shadows and the interplay of light and dark both on the exterior of buildings and on the interior. Much of her work details the paraphernalia of the wool industry. The physical isolation of these properties has created sites loaded with historical detail. She has done many hundreds of paintings of sheds, becoming, in the process, a recorder of local histories.

'The Shearing Shed.' Shearing is an activity that's embedded in the Australian mind, even for people who've never done it. The sheds themselves represent a lot of outback life.

JAN LONG

Jan Long is motivated by her stimulating environment in East Gippsland, which provides her with characters, wildlife and objects that she loves to paint. Her artworks are realistic in style, with high impact from accuracy and technical expertise that she has developed from the enormous amount of time she spends on each painting. She chooses from a variety of subjects including buildings, birds and animals, people and the countryside in all its moods and seasons. Like many artists, Jan sees a painting in the simplest of objects, from a fence post to chooks wandering about in the yard.

After teaching for many years, Jan decided in 1987 to make a full-time commitment to drawing and painting and now has more than 100 first prize awards in major exhibitions. She was included in the book *Fifty Australian Artists* and her paintings are in collections throughout Australia and overseas (including the Australian Embassy in Paris). What an achievement!

'Cattle Country.' The area painted here is the Tambo River in the high country of East Gippsland in Victoria. Can you see the rider at the far end of the cattle?

PETER MORTIMORE

Peter Mortimore has been painting for some 15 years and says that his main influences are Australian traditional painters, especially Sir Hans Heysen, George Lambert, Rupert Bunny, Tom Roberts, Arthur Streeton, Norman Lindsay and William Dobell. Tim Storrier in particular has had an enormous influence on Peter's work. Peter loves the country and delights in the sense of humour he derives from the bush. 'I think this dry humour is imparted from the struggle of living out here with fires, floods, droughts and whatever else is dished up to us,' he says. How true is that!

Peter wants his art enjoyed, not analysed. He wants to leave the viewer with a visual experience that for a moment takes them away from the worries of their own lives. The preciseness of his detail comes from his love of drawing and closeness to his subject. Peter runs painting schools, which really recharges his creativity and keeps him expressing his interpretations of our fascinating country.

'Girth's Twisted.' People on the land know it's essential to care for your horses. They're great mates. Where would Australia be without the noble horse?

WINSOME BOARD

Winsome Board has painted since early childhood when her favourite study was horses. Today, four decades later, she loves the landscapes that reflect the beauty of the land where the rainforest meets the west. For as long as she can remember, she has been fascinated with capturing the spirit of places, mysterious, dramatic or tranquil. Realistic in style, her paintings evoke a sense of presence behind the patterns of light and shade.

Winsome has held five Australian solo exhibitions and has won a number of regional art prizes. Many of her paintings are among private collections both here at home and overseas and 'Edge of the Scrub', a painting which represents the Tully area, hangs in Queensland's Parliament House. Winsome has her own gallery in Ravenshoe. Her latest passion is promoting the art of Tableland and northern artists to a wider public by using the Internet.

'The Spirit Tree.' This is at Cape York, a truly spiritual place. Termite mounds up this way can be very tall, as you can see in this painting.

ALBERT NAMATJIRA

Albert Namatjira is without doubt Australia's best known Aboriginal painter, and a man I admire greatly. Success brought him money and fame, but behind the story of this talented artist lurks a sorrowful tale of a man caught between two worlds. A struggle for recognition within white society and his pain at not always fulfilling his obligations in tribal life left him torn and in 1958 he died a broken, bitter man.

Born Elea to his parents, Namatjira was re-named Albert after his family adopted Christianity at the Hermannsburg Mission (only an hour from my home). At 13, he disappeared from the mission for six months and was taken in by the old men of the Aranda tribe to be initiated into manhood, an important ritual for Aboriginal boys. At 18 he eloped with Rubina. The cost of raising three young children found Albert working with camels carrying freight to Oodnadatta and back. Along with selling small pieces of Albert's artwork they got by, but it was a meagre existence.

In 1934 an artist, Rex Battarbee held an exhibition at the Mission. Battarbee so inspired Albert that he decided to take art lessons from him. The student quickly surpassed the teacher and the rest, as they say, is history. I can't imagine an Australia without the famous Namatjira 'ghostly gums'. These unique landscapes made him famous.

Albert had an exhibition in Melbourne in December 1938. The paintings in the exhibition were the first to bear his full signature. His work so impressed the Melbourne art world that, within three days, all 41 paintings had been sold! Albert became a celebrity, even meeting Queen Elizabeth in Canberra, but he was always relieved to go home to the desert. They dressed him up and paraded him around to dignitaries, but they were happy for him to go home and not be part of their society.

Albert was granted citizenship, a right not then extended to Aboriginal people. As a citizen he could now buy alcohol—something his friends expected him to share. By doing this he broke white man's law and in 1958 he spent three months in jail for supplying liquor to friends and relatives. Just two months after his release from jail Albert Namatjira died. They say his spirit had been broken. I wish society had treated Albert better. However, my talented old neighbour, your work lives on and your outback watercolour paintings will never be matched by anyone! Mr Namatjira, you're a true outback legend!

Albert Namatjira's grave in Alice Springs.

DID YOU KNOW ... Albert Namatjira has inspired other Aboriginal people to paint—some of whom are his own children and grandchildren.

The beauty of the bush inspired
Albert's great landscapes. In my
opinion, no one can match Albert
for capturing the real essence of
the Outback.

CHAPTER 8

GEMSTONES

When I was a kid growing up at Waite River, 250 kilometres northeast of Alice Springs, I was always intrigued with gemstones. I believed that one day I would find a big gold nugget. I used to spend lots of hours in the afternoon looking for garnet, zircons, jasper and quartz in the creek beds around our place. Not far from us was Harts Range, a great area for semi-precious gemstones. I used to search through these fields. At times I imagined I would become a jeweller and would go out and buy a tube of glue and put together necklaces, earrings and rings for my sisters and my mum as a way of saving money on birthday presents. Once I even went down to the rubbish tip at the station and found an old washing machine so I could pull out the electric motor to build a 'tumbler'. I engineered a few poles to roll, and with the fan belt from the washing machine I soon had set up something that could tumble the rocks and separate the gems from the dirt. I still have that collection today, and bringing them out from time to time brings back those memories.

We still have so many riches in outback Australia. We haven't even scraped the surface yet with our gems, our diamonds, even gold. There is still plenty of fun and adventure to be had by getting out into it. Just don't be greedy—take some pieces as samples for your collection but leave Mother Earth the way you found her.

Australia's national gem is the opal, and Australia probably contains more precious opal than the rest of the world. The big opal producers are the South Australian fields of Coober Pedy and Andamooka. Lightning Ridge in New South Wales is the source of the unique black opal.

OPALS

Opals, both uncut and polished, show a wonderful array of colours. It's like having a paintbox!

The opal is Australia's national gemstone. With its rainbow of colours, this unique gemstone derived its name from *opalus*, an ancient word meaning 'to see a play in colour'. Opals are said to contain the wonders of the skies. Aboriginal people however, believed that each of these sparkling stones housed a devil, so they had nothing much to do with them.

Hidden deep in the heart of the Outback, this elusive gem began life more than 100 million years ago when the deserts of Central Australia were a great inland sea. Opals were found mainly around the edges of a major geological formation known as The Great Artesian Basin. The mineral silica mixed with water and made a gel that seeped deep into the cracks and ridges; as the water dried out the gel became an opal. Opals are one of the few gemstones that are formed like this. They still contains 6 to 10 per cent water, a remnant of that ancient sea.

Opals occur in many forms, but the best known is the gemstone of many colours. The strength of the colours depends on the background body colour and the transparency of the stone. The body colour determines the variety of opal and has a large impact on its value. Black opal, which is black to dark grey, has the most brilliant colours and is the most valuable. White and milky opals tend to have more diffused colours because of the light background colour.

Australia has been the world's main producer of opals ever since the nineteenth century. Most of Australia's great opals have come from Lightning Ridge in New South Wales.

DID YOU KNOW ... The black opal from Lightning Ridge was so extraordinary that customers in Europe found it difficult to believe that such an opal was a natural stone!

If you turn an opal round in your hand, you'll notice that the brilliant colours seem to change. This is because light is reflected off the small cracks in the stone.

SAPPHIRES

Sapphires belong to the corundrum family of gems. Not many people realise that they come in a range of colours, including yellow, purple and red (the red ones are known as rubies). There are even clear sapphires! Corundrum is the crystalline form of aluminium oxide. After diamonds, it is the hardest natural substance. Corundrum is actually colourless—what gives the sapphire its colour are the tiny amounts of trace elements which are absorbed while the stone is being formed. Various combinations of trace elements produce different colours. Blue sapphires, the most popular colour, are formed when titanium and iron are absorbed into the crystal.

Sapphires are among the most popular of coloured stones and adorn many pieces of jewellery from small rings to royal crowns! But sapphires are also incredibly useful in industry. Sapphire crystals are found in watches and clocks, in medical and scientific equipment, laser scanners and computer circuitry. In fact, so useful are they that many places around the world actually manufacture their own sapphires!

Sapphires can be found in all states of Australia, most notably in Queensland, as well as the Northern Territory. Anakie in Queensland is one of Australia's major gemfields, ranking with the opalfields of South Australia and New South Wales. Top quality yellow sapphires are the most valuable of the Anakie gems.

Sapphire mining is now all done by machinery, and the majority of Australian sapphires end up in Thailand, which is probably the world's biggest processor and marketer of sapphires and rubies. I love sapphires because they remind me of the blue skies of the Australian Outback.

PEARLS

Above: Harvesting a pearl from an oyster farmed on the Australia's northwest coast.

Opposite: Beautiful South Sea pearls!

Thought of as tears of the gods in ancient times, pearls are regarded as the most romantic and feminine of gems. A pearl is an abnormal growth resulting from the invasion of the body of a shellfish by a tiny particle of foreign matter, such as a fine grain of sand. The particle acts as an irritant inside the shell and becomes coated with layers and layers of mother-of-pearl, which builds up to form the pearl.

The Australian commercial pearl industry dates back to the 1850s when European pearlers arrived on the west coast to seek the Australian silver lip oyster, which was, and still is, as large as any pearl shell in the world. But the pearling industry really took off in the 1880s in Western Australia and these days is worth an amazing $200 million annually!

Australian vessel owners employed Aboriginal divers early in its lively history as they were already skilled in the art of free diving and could collect the pearl shell at low tide. But hazards, such as certain marine predators and the horrible decompression illness known as the bends, took a heavy toll of pearling crews and divers in earlier decades. The Japanese were also a significant presence, diving for pearls during the 1920s. At the outbreak of World War II, pearling came to a standstill, as many Japanese were interned.

The cultured pearl industry began in the 1950s and today Western Australian pearls are regarded as the world's best. What *is* a cultured pearl? A cultured pearl is produced by a method called seeding. It involves cutting a small section of mantle from a donor oyster and placing it next to the bead which is implanted in the oyster. This grafting process allows for a sac to be formed around the bead, which in turn excretes mother-of-pearl (nacre), and forms a pearl.

The first pearl farm was established at the remote western end of the Kimberleys 420 kilometres north of Broome. It was called 'Kuri Bay'. This farm had immediate success and by the 1970s Australia was producing 60 per cent of the world's finest and largest cultured pearls. These were known as 'South Sea pearls' or 'Kuri Bay pearls'. Since then, many farms have been developed and there are now about 30 ranging from Exmouth Gulf in Western Australia to Cape York in Queensland. One of the best areas for collecting shells is Eighty Mile Beach which runs between Port Hedland and Broome.

Paspaley Pearls took over the original Pearls Pty Ltd and now have the largest and most sophisticated operation in the world. They produce nearly half of the Australian pearl harvest each year.

DID YOU KNOW ... Pearl diving today can be a very lucrative job. A top diver can gather 50 to 60 shells per dive (there is a legal requirement that these must be 120 millimetres across) and make up to eight dives per day. At $5.00 per shell they can make $2,000–$2,500.00 per day.

ORANGE GARNET

These uncut orange garnet crystals come from Harts Range in the Northern Territory.

Some orange garnets from my aunt's collection. The stone on the bottom left is a flawless seven-carat orange garnet in an emerald cut; the stone on the bottom right is eight carats. It's in a free form and is also flawless.

Some of my family mined orange garnet (hessonite and grossular) at Harts Range for about three years. My Uncle Walter found it many years ago. But quartz surrounds the garnet and it is very hard to mine, so my aunt and uncle used air compressors to run the jack hammers, Even then, they bent the hammers trying to extract the garnet, and because it is fragile it tends to shatter the gem.

So they decided to extract the garnet by hammer and chisel and unfortunately sustained a lot of fractures in the process, which meant that the majority of cutable stones were kind of small. But they did get some larger pieces and now have quite a nice collection. The photographs on this page are from my Aunty Faye's collection. I think they're pretty impressive, don't you?

My aunt and uncle also have three lovely complete crystals. These are orange, yellow and burnt orange. This garnet runs in all the autumn colours, starting from almost white to a very burnt orange. As far as we know, orange garnet or hessonite, as it it sometimes known, is only found in one place in Australia and that is at Harts Range. This is not widely known— until now that is!

DID YOU KNOW ... The orange-brown colour of hessonite garnet is from bits of manganese and iron that are absorbed by the stone as it is formed. The swirls look like honey.

DIAMONDS

Natural diamonds are formed deep in the earth's interior, at depths of at least 150 kilometres from the earth's surface. Some of Australia's first diamonds were discovered among gravel on the alluvial tin fields in Copeton in the nineteenth century. Children kept them in jars and called them 'shineys'. From very modest beginnings, Australia's diamond industry has grown and Australia now produces about one-third of the world's diamond supply.

Our main diamond fields lie in the Kimberley region of Western Australia, in stream gravels and the original host rock. Most of this is from the Argyle Diamond Mine, which commenced operations in December 1985 and is the world's biggest single producer of diamonds. Between 1992 and 1993, 32.2 mega carats of diamonds (both sorted and unsorted), and valued at $483 million, were exported out of the country.

Diamonds have also been found in South Australia. In fact, within 25 years of founding that state, diamonds were discovered on the alluvial goldfields at Echunga. In 1879 the Commissioner of Crown Lands engaged the services of G T Bean, an experienced gem digger to examine and report on the Echunga field. He recommended that a systematic search should be undertaken. Since then most diamonds found in that area were accidental discoveries while panning for gold. At Mount Kingston in the far north of South Australia, a diamond was discovered in 1894 by a small party looking for gold. Another was found in the same area, at Algebuckina in 1908. Others have since been found at Edwards Creek, about 100 kilometres south from Oodnadatta. Discoveries have been made at several localities such as Eurelia, by Stockdale Prospecting Ltd, Pine Creek, Ketchowla and Franklyn near Terowie and Karatta on Kangaroo Island.

There have been more recent discoveries and diamond mining attracts overseas investment, especially in the fields of exploration and testing. Who knows what more riches lie under the soil?

Sorting diamonds at the Argyle Diamond Mine in Western Australia.

The way the light shines through a diamond is pretty awesome. Diamonds are the hardest natural substance on earth!

DID YOU KNOW ... A diamond can only be cut by another diamond!

GOLD

From the early days of white settlement in Australia, rumours abounded about how much gold was around, but settlers had more important things on their minds, like setting up their farms, raising livestock and growing crops. Gold was found in New South Wales in 1839, but Governor Gipps made sure no one heard about it. He was afraid the convicts would rush off to search for gold, and leave the colony in a state of disarray.

It wasn't until 1851 that the gold rushes officially began here. The first goldfield was at Ophir, near Orange in the west of New South Wales. Later that year, gold was discovered near Ballarat in Victoria, an event which resulted in the Victorian Rushes, with miners prospecting all over the state. So many people poured into Melbourne that by 1861 it was Australia's largest city. The gold rushes also contributed to today's multicultural society, when Chinese prospectors arrived in 1857 to find their fortunes.

Gold was also found in Queensland, Tasmania and South Australia in the 1850s and 1860s. There was very little gold mining in the Northern Territory. When the Overland Telegraph Line between Adelaide and Darwin was being constructed in 1871, workers found gold along the way, mainly at Pine Creek. Later, gold was discovered at Arltunga some 100 kilometres east of Alice Springs. It wasn't until the 1800s that gold was found in Western Australia in the Kimberley region, the Pilbara and Coolgardie. Western Australia became the state that produced the most gold for Australia, and gold is still being mined there today.

The gold rushes really gave the young colony a push-along. In 1854, Cobb & Co established a coach service in Victoria. Roads were improved, and the first telegraph was set up between Melbourne and Williamstown. Post offices became more efficient and a steam railway (Australia's first) opened in Melbourne. But it didn't take long for the government to make miners pay a licence fee to stake a claim. It was really open to corruption with officials taking pay-offs and harassing the miners. Miners objected to the licensing system and things soon came to a head. The miners built a barricade—the Eureka Stockade—to keep the soldiers out. Early in the morning of 3 December 1854 soldiers and police stormed the stockade, resulting in the death of 24 miners and five soldiers. After this tragedy, the licence fee was abolished. The battle of Eureka Stockade is truly one of the great stories of ordinary people fighting for their rights!

Panning for gold in the early days of the gold rushes. Some miners made a fortune, but many went away from the goldfields with nothing.

Those days are long gone, but gold has lost none of its appeal. Today, Australia is one of the biggest producers of gold in the world. Most modern gold mines are open-cut mines, but underground mining is also important. Kalgoorlie in Western Australia is probably the best known gold mining region in the country. In fact, Western Australia accounts for a whopping three-quarters of Australia's gold. What a record!

DID YOU KNOW ... The unit used to weigh gold is called the troy ounce. I promise you that I didn't name it! One troy ounce equals a little over 31 grams.

This old gold mine at Kalgoorlie provides a stark contrast with the evening sky.

An open-cut gold mine at Tennant Creek in the Northern Territory. Gold mining employs many thousands of Australians.

CHAPTER 9

ADVENTURES

The Outback is a vast wonderland. I have spent my whole life in the Outback and had many adventures there, and I want to share just a few of them with you. From my earliest years, I learned plenty of bush skills from my father and from my Aboriginal friends, but nothing prepares you for the unexpected like, well, the unexpected!

If you're ever out bush, there are a few golden rules you should remember. The first is to tell people where you're going, so if you do get lost or don't arrive somewhere that you're expected, people will know where to start looking for you. Another absolutely critical rule is to take some water with you, as it's not easy to find in the enormous and remote desert, and believe me, you can dehydrate very quickly on a hot day. And wear a hat, because the sun gets really fierce—even in winter. If you're really smart, you'll take some sunscreen with you too. Good gear is another must. Walking boots are compulsory. The ground out there can be tough and the last thing you need is to damage your feet by wearing the wrong boots.

But don't let these rules put you off. There's so much excitement out there that you'd be mad to miss out on it. Just remember that the elements can be relentless and it pays to respect them. I'd encourage you to visit the Outback at least a few times in your life. It's the heart and soul of Australia.

This is me in my trusty helicopter mustering a herd of wild camels. They are very intelligent animals.

TIDAL WATERFALLS

Tiger sharks are not uncommon off the Western Australian coast.

Besides my own central part of Australia, the Kimberley has to be one of the last frontiers. There's not much commercial fishing in this area, so the place is wild with crocodiles, sharks and lots of venomous box jellyfish. Swimming is not the number one sport here! Although I have lived in the Outback all my life, travelling through the Buccaneer Archipelago at the top end of the Kimberley region with my film crew totally opened up my eyes to this glorious part of Australia. One of my favourite adventures was jumping the waterfalls up here on a jet ski. A horizontal waterfall. A tidal waterfall.

With 8 metre tides, the ebb and flow of the coastal waters between the rocky passages can be horrendously dangerous. Every odd hour the action is at is peak, so you might make it in one way and find you can't get back out the other. I jumped through it six times once to film it and I didn't have any security harness or anything to pick me out of the whirlpools. These can be 4 or 5 metres wide. One goes left to right as you go through, and the other right to left like matching cyclones, just waiting to gobble me up should I make a wrong move.

Both sides of this turbulent water are a hangout for lots of fish, crocs and sharks. If I'd fallen off, even if I hadn't drowned from being pulled under the water by the currents, I wouldn't have made it out. It was the most nerve-racking time I have had riding a jet ski. The last time I went through at its peak at high tide and the jet ski took off 3 metres in the air. I did it on a waveblaster, and it surely was one of the most adrenaline-driving stunts I've ever done. I even lost my sunglasses as I hit off one of the jumps. Maybe there's a crocodile or shark up there with a belly full of sunglasses. Or perhaps a big fish is wearing them, thinking he's pretty cool!

This photograph was taken when I was about 200 metres from the tidal waterfall. My heart was racing because no one had ever jumped them before on a jet ski and falling off could have been fatal.

FISHING

I'm a pretty lucky bloke being able to fly all around the top end of Australia. One of the most memorable times was fishing with my mate and fellow flying companion, Steve Groves. The beautiful thing about a helicopter is that you can get to spots that even commercial fishermen can't get to.

This particular day, we landed on a levy bank just wide enough to hold the helicopter skids, in an area where the water flows through to the open sea. Barramundi are the game fish up there and this spot was supposed to be chock full of the big ones.

Steve and I must have looked a sight—two blokes throwing lures out, between two helicopters perched on either side of them. But within 20 minutes we each took eight big barramundi, each weighing between 10 and 20 kilograms. Steve stole the show with a 25 kilogram monster. We only took home enough to eat and threw the rest back in.

I remember my feeling of excitement, because I can be a very impatient fisherman and if I don't catch something in five minutes, I want to go somewhere else, but this was the best fishing I've ever done. After that we parked our helicopters a couple of kilometres away on a shelly little beach when the tide was down and speared about 20 mud crabs. When we got home, we had three or four 10 kilogram barramundi and a fat bag full of crabs. What a feast!

Fishermen can go out for weeks on end trying to catch these trophies but Steve and I had them all in three hours—one of the best reasons for having a flying fishing vehicle, I reckon.

HELICOPTER FAILURE

This is me and my chopper near my home. I was lucky enough to have been taught to fly choppers by Charles Pooley; he taught me to remain cool under pressure, follow the correct procedures and make instant decisions.

Once I was flying with my film crew, while my mate Steve Groves was flying along beside me in another Bell 473B1. We were filming the Big Wet in the Northern Territory. It was the year of the Katherine Floods and the water was chest high for hundreds of miles inland. I was taking a girl to see her boyfriend at Dundee Beach, southwest of Darwin. I was about 10 kilometres into the middle of a big paperbark swamp when I noticed my manifold pressure had dropped off and I was losing power and rpm; no matter how hard I tried to lower my collective and pick up rpm it was to no avail. My air speed was quickly declining from 70 knots to 60 knots, so I radioed Steve and reported a May Day! The power was bleeding off fast and I soon hit 50 knots. There were huge 15-metre trees all around and not much room to get my chopper in anywhere.

I decided to put it in the swamp before all my air speed was lost. I was down to 45 knots, so I picked four trees to take her down between. At 10 metres above the water, I flared out, judging trees only by centimetres. I didn't want to run it on, as the skids may have hooked on the reeds in the water and tipped the chopper over. I cushioned the landing very lightly, my skids hit the water and we sank down slowly! Luckily it was one of my better landings. I obviously had someone looking after me. I shot out of my side and pulled myself through the belly-button high water to get the girl clear of danger. When the chopper hit the water, the long and short shafts of the tail rotor broke, so I had no choice but to find a way to get it lifted out. Steve hovered above the water some 50 metres away. I lifted my passenger into Steve's chopper and he flew off. Waiting in the swamp, on my own and with no radio contact, was even scarier than taking the chopper down. Hearing the splashing and the sounds of what I thought were crocs looking for a good feed, I kept doing 360° turns with a big log.

Finally, help arrived and my cameraman, Simon Menzies, was lowered into the swamp to get some memories of this unusual expedition. We pulled the chopper out—and a few leeches from Simon's legs. Do you know it cost about $45,000 to get her flying again. But at least I'm still here to tell the tale.

I'll never forget going down in that paperbark swamp. And like falling off a bike, or a bull, I learned to get right back on again. As soon as my chopper was fixed I was out exploring more of our Australian Outback.

Looking at the control panel on the inside of the helicopter and the hills outside, there's a real three-dimensional feel about it.

CLIMBING THE HOME RANGE

The Western MacDonnells are beautiful, but as you can see, the rocks are quite forbidding. Always be properly prepared when going rock climbing.

This story comes from close to home in the Western MacDonnells, only 20 kilometres away. I went 'mountain climbing' with my cousin. We disobeyed the number one rule of climbing—always have the right gear, especially boots with a good grip. We took our ordinary work boots. Two-thirds of the way up the 'walk' turned into a frightening climb. The wind was blowing like nothing else and I was soon clinging onto the sides of trees that were growing out of the rock. I slipped and was hanging by a branch. I couldn't go down because it was too far to the next branch and I couldn't go up because my boots wouldn't hold. The only thing I could do was to crawl up a tree trunk, put my knee into the trunk and dig my claws into the pores in the rock. We were at about an angle of around 75°. It took us an hour to get the 5 metres we needed to get a secure hold.

When we reached the top of that summit, it was the most spectacular view. Amburla Station was visible in the distance and we savoured the view for some time. We thought it would be clean sailing all the way down but we had another think coming. Soon my heart was pumping out of my skin as I found myself on another rock ledge where I couldn't go down or back up. Once again I was on my stomach and hands sliding down backwards until I hit a solid jagged rock sticking out. I sprained my ankle rather badly and had to take the long way round to the bottom. The round trip took a total of eight hours. But I learned a big lesson that day—have the right gear, because I could have lost my life doing something silly.

MUD BOG RACING

I've raced motorbikes across the Outback all my life. Mustering stock, and as a kid looking for adventure I was always on a bike looking for excitement. As with mountain climbing, you need to have the right gear. Make sure you always have your helmet. I would've saved myself a lot of injuries if I'd learned that lesson a bit earlier. The same goes for boots. I've broken my ankles twice on motorbikes, and both times could have been prevented if I'd been wearing good motorbike boots. When we were kids, we'd cull kangaroos from our bikes. I never liked shooting them; I prefer to catch them and shift them to a new area. Anyway, catching a kangaroo on a motorbike is easier said than done. The idea is to follow them for a while at about 60 kilometres per hour, until they are so tired you can reach out, grab them by the tail, stop the bike and pick them up.

It was this sort of experience I took with me when I entered the Darwin Mud Bog races in 1999. I had a Yamaha YZ250 two stroke and was prepared for anything. Little did I expect a mud bath. Racing around the track, competitors leave the place a series of mud bog pits. Your bike has mud coming up as high as its seat, and well over the exhaust pipes. Jumps are up to 10 metres along a kidney-shaped track. I was feeling quite embarrassed as 10,000 spectactors watched me and my bike conk out with mud overload. I dragged the bike out of the mud and water and pushed it back to the starting point. My support team, Steve and Gerry, cleaned her up and helped me back into another round for another chance at the title later in the night. We covered all the openings with electrical tape and sprayed anything electrical with CRC so no water would slow us down.

I entered the next heat, went a bit crazy and won it outright, with some good luck from the patron saint of Mud. I soon was covered with mud but happy as a pig in its sty. I won the third heat, and then the finals with the fastest time of the night. If this was not my happiest time on a motorbike, it surely was my muddiest.

This is me preparing for the mud bog races, before I got muddy!

HORSEBITE

My most action-packed memory of chasing wild horses was when I was on my motorbike climbing the hills just below Mount Hay on our property Amburla, in a paddock we call The Valley. There's lots of pebbly rocks up there, and it's very hard to ride a motorbike across it. On this particular day, there were about 30 wild brumbies running up the valley. They were eating out the paddock, so we had to move them. We had a helicopter in the air, and a friend and me on motorbikes.

We had a big mob not far from The Valley waterbore, when a white stallion decided to break away and bolt for the hills. Nothing was going to stop him. There were trees, gullies, rocks and creekbeds and I was flat out on the motorbike among them. He was a beauty and I was determined to get him back. Within minutes we were at 60 kilometres an hour; trees were zipping past half a metre from either side of the handlebars, so judgment was critical. The stallion jumped and darted between trees. He was clever. All the time he could see the hills of his beloved Mount Hay. On one of his charges for the hills, I cut him off and wheeled him back out on the black soil plain. Then I jumped a 3 metre gully, which the horse also cleared, and when we got across, I was very close.

Just as I was right beside his head, he turned and bit me on the shoulder. He bit hard, and the harder he bit, the more I put down the throttle. The more I put down the throttle, the more he bit me. Eventually I pulled away and he cut right across in front of me. I hit the brakes trying not to go over him, but just then I saw a big ugly rock right in front of me. I shot 4 metres in the air and hit the ground; the bike came down on top of me. I was glad I was wearing a helmet; otherwise I may have been killed. Grazed and bruised, the first thing that came into my head, funnily enough, was Banjo Paterson's legendary poem *The Man from Snowy River*. Banjo knew that once a wild stallion wants to head somewhere, there's very little you can do about it.

I've had so many adventures on my motorbike! It's a real friend. In this photo, I was doing some stunt riding. When you're on a bike, take my advice and wear a helmet.

A BABY CALF

This was quite an emotional adventure, and one that I'm proud of because I know if I hadn't done something, this calf would never have been born. We had only just started the Brahman stud and we had a lot of expensive cows about the place. One day on a bore run, I saw a pregnant Brahman cow lying down near the water trough and she was in pain. She was on her belly trying to give birth to her calf and was having big trouble. Under normal circumstances both mother and calf would have died. The calf's shoulders were just too big to get through.

I had seen Dad take care of this type of situation a few times when I was growing up so I went for it. I got a mob of water from the trough and put it around the outside of her vagina, to make pulling the calf out easier. His legs were stuck and his head was coming between his front legs, so I had to put my arm inside to push his head back and fold the legs back under. Once the head was back in and the legs were folded under, I could put my hand back in, grab him by the ears and start to help the cow push him out again. It took nearly an hour, and the cow was totally exhausted with little energy for any more contractions. With one last heave, I fell backwards, the calf on top of me. I was covered in blood and mucus, not to mention all the afterbirth. The calf's mouth was on my chin and his big eyes were open and looking up at me. He couldn't breathe because his tongue was turned inside out. So I lifted him up by his back legs and held him right out so his mouth was pointing straight down to the ground. I pumped on his stomach a bit until all this mucus came out of his mouth and he could breathe again.

The exhausted mother looked at me; she seemed to say 'thank you'. You shouldn't handle newborns too much as the mother smells her own afterbirth, and knows the calf is her own. But I picked the calf up and lay it down alongside her. At first she did nothing. I walked away to allow her a bit of security, watching from a distance for the next hour. Finally she started licking him. I brought her a bucket of water and she had a long drink, and I also picked her some grass. Eventually she start nibbling. It was getting dark and I had to get back, but the next morning at daylight I went to see if they were all right. And they were fine. The calf was staggering on his legs but he was drinking from his mother's udders. His tummy was pushed right out so he'd had a good feed. They both survived my first veterinary experience. I named that calf Amburla Apollo and today he is one of our top stud bulls.

We are really proud of our Brahman stock. Hard work has meant that today we have an excellent stud farm.

I think Brahman calves are very cute. This one walks happily behind his mother at our property. What should I name this little bloke?

LOST IN THE BUSH

Another lesson I learned early in life is to always tell someone where you are heading. This little adventure began when I was on a bore run and my motorbike broke down, but no one had a clue where I was. I had left that morning without leaving a note. On a million acre spread this can be problematic. Where do you start looking? As for me, I had a 30-kilometre walk home.

I had been riding along quite happily on the northern boundary checking the fences, when I hit an ant hill doing 60 kilometres. The bike stopped dead, I went over the handlebars and the bike followed, hitting me in the lower back. Mum hates motorbikes and you can see why. I was winded and the bike was out of action, so I began walking home, feeling very sore and sorry. The second rule of the Outback is always have some water with you. I didn't, and it was 10 kilometres to the nearest bore. I grew up with Aboriginal kids and had been on some pretty long walks living off the land; and my father had taught me a few things about survival too. I knew about following the sun in the day and the stars at night.

At this time, the sun was about halfway down to the west and the road was about 15 kilometres that way, but I wanted to find that bore, so I kept the sun at a nine o'clock position and headed through the scrub. By the time I got there I would have killed for a drink of water. I was also starving, as I had skipped breakfast that morning. I found a disused dirt road on the property and followed it for four hours, finding bits of bush tucker along the way, like witchetty bushes, bush apples from mulga bushes, and wild coconuts from bloodwood trees. I also found some wild bananas. Eating this bush food kept me from getting delirious in the hot summer sun. Had I left a message with my family, I could have stayed at that bore and waited for someone to come along and pick me up. It was a valuable lesson to learn.

Amburla Station, near our main stockyards, is where I was headed after my bike broke down 30 kilometres from home!

THE ROYAL FLYING DOCTOR SERVICE

Those of us who live in the Outback have adventures every day, just doing the regular things we do to maintain our properties and farms. Many stations are quite isolated so it's good to know that if an accident occurs, help is just a radio call away. It wasn't always like this. The Royal Flying Doctor Service began in 1928, when it was set up by the Reverend Dr John Flynn, who wanted to provide people in the Outback with what he called 'a mantle of safety'. You can read about John Flynn on page 71. The Flying Doctors now cover a whopping 80 per cent of Australia!

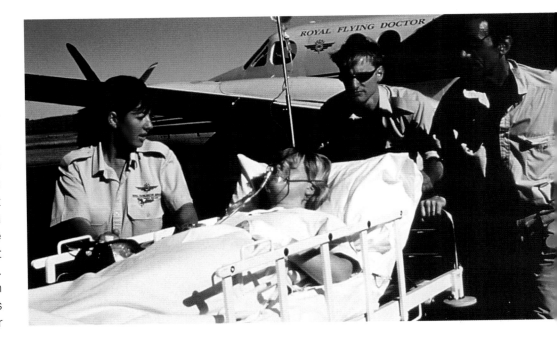

The Flying Doctors are dedicated professional men and women who bring much needed medical services to even the most remote parts of the country. What adventures they must have!

The Flying Doctors have adventures every day too, flying all over the outback to assist sick or injured people. When it began, the RFDS had only one bi-plane and one doctor. Today it has 45 aircraft, 18 different bases and about 350 people on staff. And what's more, they cover an area of Australia that is more than 7 million square kilometres! Now that's a big waiting room.

The RFDS transports sick and injured people to the nearest hospital. But it also holds clinics, covering all sorts of health issues. For example, there is a clinic especially for new mums, so that they can get help with their babies. Clinics are held in all manner of locations, like mines or homesteads. Everyone in the area finds out when the clinic is on, and heads off to see the doctors and nurses there. It's also a time when you can catch up with some of your more remote neighbours. The Flying Doctors are well and truly part of outback adventures.

I remember once a stockman was checking out one of the horse paddock fences when he ran over a 2 metre king brown snake. It flung itself upon the bike and wrapped itself around the exhaust. As the stockman changed gears, the snake struck his foot. The Flying Doctors arrived soon after our call and took him safely to Alice Springs Hospital. The doctors said it was lucky that most of the venom went into the boot leather!

DID YOU KNOW ... Even if you're in the most remote location, the Flying Doctors can be there in no more than 90 minutes!

CHAPTER 10

LIVING OFF
THE LAND

The Australian continent covers over 7 million square kilometres and consists of a diverse range of environments, from the tropical coast of the top, the arid deserts of the centre and the woodlands of the east. The selection of fruits, flowers, vegetables, animals, birds, reptiles, herbs and spices that are native to our country across these environments is referred to as bush tucker.

Before European settlement, Aboriginal Australians ate rich and balanced diets of seasonal fruits, nuts, roots, vegetables, meats and fish. In fact, Aboriginal people have been eating bush tucker for more than 50,000 years. Exactly what was eaten varied according to what was available in particular areas. It also depended on the seasons, diversity of land, soil, flora and weather conditions. There are hundreds of varieties of fruits, nuts and vegetables found on bushes, shrubs and vines throughout the country. But if you don't know what you're looking for, leave them alone as some can make you very sick.

Today in some areas, bush foods are still collected and used in the same way as many Aboriginal communities traditionally used them. Because they understood the land and what it can yield, Aboriginal people have successfully lived off the land for tens of thousands of years. With this in mind, it is crucial for non-Aboriginal Australians to develop a better understanding of how to preserve this great land of ours.

Over the last few years contemporary Australian cuisine has introduced many indigenous Australian foods into restaurants, and many chefs are developing an interest in products unique to their environment seeking to diversify with 'new' tastes and combinations. This includes meats such as kangaroo, emu and crocodile. Jams, sauces and chutneys are made with wild plums and fruits. A number of desserts are also made with native fruits, nuts and seeds.

This chapter gives you an insight into some of the diversity of the bush tucker spread throughout Australia, and I also have a look at some of the key implements and tools used by Aboriginal people of the past and present.

I hope our native bush foods continue to play an active role in today's society. The potential to market our unique foods to the rest of the world is huge. Bush tucker is yet another example of how great this land is.

These large stones were used for grinding seeds. The stones are dated at over 10,000 years old.

TUCKER TOOLS

Baskets and digging sticks were crucial tools in the collection of food for Aboriginal communities. Aboriginal women made baskets from various types of grasses, reeds, bark and string manufactured from plant fibre and animal hair. Baskets were used to carry tools, personal items and food. The digging stick was not only used to dig up a variety of edible plants, such as yams, it was also used to hunt small animals.

Today the skills of making baskets and collecting food are passed on to the children within each community. This keeps the knowledge alive. I hope this continues and that we can inspire the younger generation to learn more of the rich culture of our land.

Aboriginal people have long used **spears** for hunting. In fact, wooden spears are some of the oldest hunting implements used by Aboriginal men. The Aboriginal hunter used his spear as a long distance precision weapon by extending his throwing arm with the use of a spear thrower. (In some areas this is called a woomera.)

Each man had a collection of spears, each spear intended for a different purpose. Some spears were weapons. Others were for hunting game, fish and turtles; others were used to punish those who broke tribal law. I have a few friends who still hunt with spears, especially when they want fish for dinner!

When I was growing up, I had my own spear, although I'm glad I had my mum's cooking at home because I was not a great hunter back then; but it was good practice for the javelin event at the school athletics.

The **boomerang** is the 'Swiss army knife' of Aboriginal Australia because of its remarkable diversity. This icon represents thousands of years of tradition for Aboriginal people, from ceremonial rituals to hunting. It was certainly an important tool in the food chain. The oldest known boomerang found in Australia has been dated at 10,000 years old, indicating Aboriginal people's long association with it.

The favoured wood for boomerangs in the Centre is the mulga. I like the mulga tree—it also provides good wood for campfires and it gives stock a strong source of protein during droughts. Boomerangs tend to be flat on one side and round on the other. The turn in the line of the boomerang gives it aerodynamic properties. The returning boomerang, from eastern Queensland and Central Australia, shares its aeronautical properties with the discus and the helicopter (my favourite way of getting about to see this great land).

The boomerang was used for hunting, fire-making, digging, musical accompaniment, skinning and gutting prey. Each community holds its own stories of how it is used. Some use it for punishment, or in burial rituals. Boomerangs can be distinctively patterned, or unadorned, or coated with ochre. The distinctive patterns usually formed a decoration, and often had religious significance.

I wonder if you knew that the shape of Parliament House in Canberra is modelled on two boomerangs? It just shows how much a part of our culture the boomerang really is.

The **woomera** is made of hollow wood. Its main task is to make spears go faster. A woomera is placed at the end of a spear to give more leverage when thrown. It is also used as a knife, chisel, engraver and digging stick. Men used the woomera when hunting, as the speed of the spear was crucial in maiming or killing their prey. A good woomera was worth its weight in gold!

Shields provided protection from clubs, boomerangs and spears, but they were also used in traditional Aboriginal society in ceremonial warfare. This ceremony allowed for the settlement of disputes without loss of life. Clubs and boomerangs were also used in such combat.

There are two types of shield—a parrying shield and a broad shield. Shaped into a concave appearance, these shields had a handle in the middle of the rear hollow. The convex side was often ornamented with lines, artwork and other decorations.

Like many tools, **clubs** had multiple purposes in Aboriginal communities. They were used for warfare, food collection, hunting game and on ceremonial occasions. They also made excellent walking sticks. Club shapes and sizes varied dramatically from region to region. Some were the size of a walking stick, others were much smaller. The club heads also differed in shapes and sizes.

With a natural grained exterior, clubs are generally left undecorated. They have their own distinctive design because of the natural grain wood. In some areas, the leaves of the sandpaper fig was used to smooth down the texture of the wood.

DID YOU KNOW ... Food collected by the women provided the bulk of the daily diet of Aboriginal people. Women were better providers of food than the men. Sometimes the men would go out to spear or capture an animal, but they often came back empty handed.

BUSH TUCKER

The Kakadu plum has the
highest known source of
natural vitamin C in the
world. One plum is believed
to have more Vitamin C
than 10–12 oranges.

BUSH BANANAS

There are two types of bush bananas in Australia. One comes from tropical rainforest areas; the other is widely distributed throughout Australia, particularly in the central drier regions of the outback. Many times out mustering I have quenched my thirst with this magic little fruit. One of my favourites.

The tropical bush (or native) bananas grow in sunny, well-watered areas such as creek banks and on the fringes of forests. This banana looks like one you'd buy in a fruit market, but the flesh has a number of inedible black seeds. The pulp, rich in Vitamin C, is best roasted; it has a sweet taste and a sticky texture. When cooking the native banana, it's best to wrap it in the broad green leaves of the tree; this protects it from ash.

The other type of bush banana looks very different from the tropical species and is found in Australia's arid zones. I see heaps of these bush bananas in the area around my place as they thrive in dry conditions. They are rich in thiamine and have long been a popular Aboriginal bush food.

The casing of the fruit can be eaten raw and tastes similar to sour green peas. However, when they are young, they just melt in your mouth. The leaves are light yellow and the inside is filled with flat seeds and white strands. The flower of the vine can also be sucked for its sweet nectar. This bush banana also tastes best cooked in ashes. It's a very versatile plant— Aboriginal people eat the leaves, flowers, shoots and seeds. I like them raw.

BUSH TOMATO

Bush tomatoes grow wild in Australia's arid centre and are more plentiful after rain or fire. They are pretty funny looking things and some look more like dried up raisins than tomatoes. Aboriginal people loved them, and when in season they made up nearly half of their diet. They are sun-dried on the bush and are still hand harvested in some areas in the traditional manner.

Today, restaurants specialising in bush tucker serve bush tomatoes as an accompaniment to native meats such as kangaroo and emu. Bush tomatoes are sold in both dried and in powdered form and are used as flavouring for casseroles, pizza bases or in pasta sauces.

Australian native plants have a long history of use by indigenous Australians and now with interest in commercial cultivation, the rest of us are starting to see native foods in shops. Fantastic I say—another way to show the world how unique our beautiful country is!

The kangaroo apple is a relative of the bush tomato. The fruit ripen from green to yellow to red.

BUNYA BUNYA NUTS

The bunya pine trees are a great Australian icon. They grow incredibly tall, making them easily recognisable even from quite a distance. The female cones on the bunya pine tree grow very large (they can be as big as a football) and each contains approximately 50 to 100 large 'nuts'. The cones are usually formed once every three years, causing a huge bumper crop to fall from the tree when ripe. The seeds are eaten raw or roasted in hot ashes. To remove the nuts, the outer skin must be peeled away from the ripened cones. Cooked nuts taste similar to European chestnuts.

In the 1850s and 1860s, Aboriginal people held bunya bunya nut celebrations in the Bunya Mountains, and hundreds of people from various tribes joined in the festivities. It was a time when tribal differences were set aside and important rituals and initiations were conducted.

These days you can find bunya bunya nuts in select supermarkets. Bunya nuts can be used in everything from casseroles to biscuits. I'm told that the flavour of the nuts greatly improves if they are left in the bottom of the fridge for months.

ABOVE: The bunya nut tree, *Araucaria bidwillii*, can reach a height of 36 metres!
BELOW: Bunya bunya nuts

QUANDONG

This plant is undoubtedly one of the most popular wild Outback fruits. Ripened fruit becomes a bright red then black, with the inner flesh of the plum covering a central stone. The plums are eaten raw and taste a bit like rhubarb. I don't like rhubarb very much so the quandong is not my favourite fruit!

Early European settlers quickly learned from the Aboriginal people, and began stewing quandongs for desserts and puddings. They also used the inner nut of the fruit as counters in Chinese chequers. Aboriginal people strung the seeds, coloured them with ochre and wore them as body ornaments and necklaces.

The seeds also have strong medicinal qualities. When ground down and mixed with water, they are said to heal skin sores and treat rheumatism.

TROY'S TIP

The leaves of the quandong tree can be burnt to get rid of mosquitoes, providing a good alternative to commercial preparations. Remember this when you go camping.

DID YOU KNOW ... In the nineteenth century it was illegal to cut bunya pines on Crown lands because they were an important food source for Aboriginal people. They are said to have buried the nuts in mud to improve the taste and make them sweeter.

Grevilleas are among the most popular of Australian native plants. They produce a sweet nectar enjoyed by both people and birds!

YAMS

The term 'yam' is often loosely applied to any underground storage organ, but the fruit of the *Dioscorea* vine are the true yams. Yams taste like potatoes to me and are among my favourite bush tucker! Yams have long been an important plant food for many Aboriginal communities. There are numerous edible species in Australia. These include the long yam (parsnip or pencil yam), the native yam, the round (cheeky yam), the desert yam (bush potato), and the Kalumburu yam from a small area of the Kimberleys.

The round yam is poisonous unless prepared properly. Because it can burn the mouth, it's also called the cheeky yam. Aboriginal people boiled it, grated it and then soaked it for 10 hours before cooking it again. Such an effort for just one meal! But they must have been tasty because the yam tops were replanted so that more would grow.

The long yam is whitish-brown. It can be eaten raw but is more palatable roasted over hot coals. The desert yam usually appears after rainfall. The bulbs of the root system are found about half a metre underground, with each plant producing several bulbs. I have dug up hundreds over the years. They're delicious. The Kalumburu yam, also known as the bush potato, is large and lumpy.

In the 1950s, scientists discovered that certain yams contain hormonal substances. They are now used to combat a variety of diseases from chronic fatigue to lupus. So when I get tired, I'll go yam hunting to get some energy!

HONEY ANTS

These ants sure know how to work together to get the job done. There are two types of honey ants in the nest, and each type has an important role in the production of honey. The ones on the surface are the 'feeders' or 'workers'. They take the nectar back to their mates who are the storers. The storers put on all the weight; with their enlarged tummies, they can become the size of a marble. The storers also get to hide out in tunnels down in the earth. What a life—lazing around all day, sleeping and getting fat! You can see the honey in

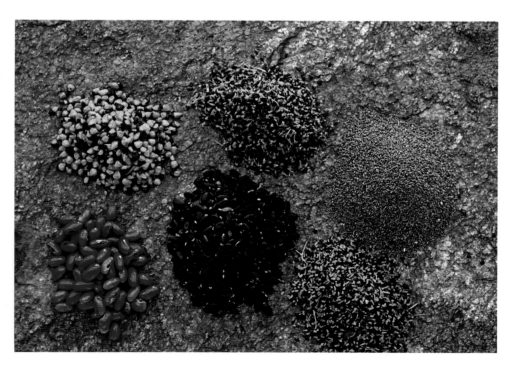

Some of the fruits of the Australian desert.

the enlarged stomach of the storer; honey is regurgitated for the workers to feed on if necessary.

Honey ants are only found in the arid areas northeast and northwest of Alice Springs, which is one of the reasons that Aboriginal people considered them a delicacy. The sweet honey from their abdomens is sucked out and makes a tasty treat. I've tried it a few times and it's delicious.

GOANNA

Gould's goanna is known by many names, including 'the racehorse goanna' or 'monitor', for its ability to take off quickly. It is found through almost all of Australia and was a staple in the diet of many Aboriginal communities. It is still considered an important bush tucker in some areas. I think it's the best tasting reptile.

The best time to catch a goanna is to surprise it while it is foraging, as its attention is focused on digging for prey. The goanna leaves a trail, which is a snake-like track with claw marks on either side. Aboriginal people can read them like a map.

The traditional way to cook a goanna is over ashes or hot coals. The white oily meat tastes similar to chicken meat. In some areas where the goanna is a totem, Aboriginal people honour it. Because it is sacred to them, it does not form part of their diet. If you ever try to catch a goanna or perentie (the goanna's larger relation), be careful, as they have very sharp claws and teeth and can inflict serious wounds.

TROY'S TIP

When preparing the goanna to eat, check the insides for eggs. These are prized by Aboriginal people for their nutritional value.

DID YOU KNOW ... The larvae found inside the leafy nest of a green ant is said to help relieve cold and flu symptoms. It would be good if it prevented them, hey?

WITCHETTY GRUB

When you mention the words 'witchetty grub' most people screw up their faces as if they've eaten something horrible. Yet the witchetty grub is one of the most well known bush foods in Australia, which is pretty impressive considering it is only found in a small area of the central outback in the Northern Territory. The first time I ate one was when I was about eight years old. I watched with disgust as Dad put a raw one in his mouth, but Dad cooked one on the barbecue for me and I discovered it tasted a bit like peanut butter.

The grubs are collected from the root system of the witchetty bush, a species of wattle tree. The word 'witchetty' comes from 'witjuti' the Arabana Aborigines' word for that particular wattle. They can also be found in some eucalyptus species, such as bloodwoods. With an axe or sharp knife an entrance is made in the roots of the tree and the grub is removed with a hooked stick or a piece of wire. I have hunted them on many occasions with my Aboriginal friends in gum trees in creek beds.

The witchetty grub has a hard head with a soft caterpillar-like body. The grub is white and can grow to the size of a man's thumb. The whole grub is edible raw, but I prefer it cooked. Some people think it has a buttery taste eaten raw; when it's cooked, it tastes kind of like scrambled eggs, bacon or pork crackling. Witchetty grubs are a true bush treat.

FRESHWATER YABBY

In inland lagoons, waterholes, dams, billabongs and creeks you are sure to find a variety of freshwater yabbies. I used to hunt them when I was a kid sometimes getting a good nip for my troubles, but it was worth it because it's a great way to spend time with your mates.

You can catch yabbies by attaching a piece of meat on a string and dangling it in the water. When the yabby feeds on it, it is gently pulled to the surface and scooped out. Yabbies can also be caught by traps, or speared. Some are the size of a crayfish (about 25 centimetres) and provide a hearty meal for the catcher. They should be boiled, preferably in salt water, until the flesh is white. The tail end is eaten and its meat is very sweet.

The scientific name, *Cheerax destructor*, refers to the yabby's habit of burrowing into levee banks and dam walls where they can cause considerable damage. They tend to hibernate in mud burrows from June to August. Pollution, over-clearing of land and introduced predators have had an adverse effect on the yabby population, but they are now commercially farmed and are offered as delicacies in restaurants.

BILLY TEA

One of the most important things a bloke can have after a long day out working in the bush is a cuppa. Believe me, when you spend a day out mustering or generally working the land, you've earned it. There is nothing better than sitting around a campfire at the end of the day with a cup of billy tea, telling a few tall tales.

Billy tea is brewed in the bush in a metal wire-handled tin, or 'billy', over an open fire. There are two versions as to how it came by its name. One is that it came from tins of French soup called *bouillie*. The empty cans were then used on the fire to brew tea in. The other theory is that the billy comes from an Aboriginal word 'billa' that means creek or river.

TROY DANN'S BILLY TEA

Boil the water on the top side of the fire just a little way in so the flames are downwind and there are a few around it (this prevents you from engulfing it with smoke and ash, which changes the taste). After it's boiled, lift it out of the fire, and for an average sized tin, put a good metric handful of tea leaves. Just before it overflows, take it off to let it settle. Enjoy!

DAMPER

Damper or 'bush bread' is best enjoyed straight out of the fire with some butter and golden syrup. Unbelievable! It may be baked on the open fire or in a regular oven. As is typical of hand-me-down recipes, there are many different versions of it. Here's the Troy Dann version for you to try.

INGREDIENTS

4 cups self-raising flour
dash of salt
30 grams butter (optional)
1 cup powdered milk
½ to 1 cup of water

METHOD

A good damper is all in the cooking—not too hot, not too cold! Once you have a lot of burnt coals from your campfire, dig a hole just bigger than the camp oven a metre or two away. Now sprinkle about one and a half shovels full of coals into the bottom of the hole, then set your damper in the oven on top. Now sprinkle another two loads across the top allowing for some to drop around the sides. Leave it for about 30–40 minutes or until it has a nice even brown crust to it. Get the butter and syrup ready and enjoy!

Freshwater turtles were traditionally cooked in an oven of hot coals made deep in the earth. I've had the opportunity to eat them a few times, but I like them alive, so I haven't. They say they taste a lot like chicken and are considered great bush tucker.

DID YOU KNOW ...
The leaves of the sandpaper fig were once used to polish tools. They are still used to clean pots.

DID YOU KNOW ...
The ruby saltbush is very common in the outback and is often found growing at the base of trees. In the MacDonnell Ranges just near my home, Aboriginal people used to soak the fruits and drink them as a sweetened tea.

TROY'S TIP ...

Make sure you rub some flour inside the oven before placing the dough inside it, to stop it from burning. For an even fancier damper sprinkle half a packet of sultanas into the ingredients. We call this the spotted dog! One more thing, if you add some light beer, it helps the damper to rise!

The fruits of the hopbush were used by early European settlers to brew beer.

PICTURE CREDITS

The green and golden bell frog is one of Australia's prettiest frogs. With its gold body and bronze gold stripes with a dash of turquoise on its groin, it's a true Aussie!

The author and publishers thank the following people and organisations for the use of their photographs and illustrations:

Loretta Barnard: pages 15, 38, 71 (bottom), 90, 75 (top), 95 (bottom), 101 (top), 118, 124
Winsome Board: page 89
Hans Boessem: pages 4-5, 17, 20, 21, 25, 28, 29, 34-37, 40, 42, 43, 54-55, 58, 59, 60 (bottom), 61 (bottom), 62, 63 (bottom), 64, 65, 66, 67, 68-69, 102-3, 106, 110 (top), 112, 113, 114, 123 (top)
Peter Browne: page 85
Braham Costello, Costello's, Perth: page 99 (bottom)
Barbara Dann: page 46
Suzanne Farmer: pages 52, 60 (top), 91
Beau Golden: pages 70, 78 (centre)
Marli Kelly: page 73 (top), 73 (bottom left)
Di King: page 84
Faye Lavender: pages 92-3, 94, 95 (top) 98
Connell Lee: page 83
Bill Leimbach (for Becker Entertainment & Outback Legend Productions): pages 2, 5 (top), 6, 11 (bottom), 19, 104 (bottom), 105, 109, 125 (top)
Jan Long: page 87
Peter Mortimore: page 88
Outback Legend Productions: pages 3, 5, 7, 72, 75 (centre), 110-11, 126 (bottom)
Paspaley Pearls, Darwin: pages 96, 97
Pest Animal Control CRC, Canberra: pages 13, 14
Christine Porter: page 86
Greg Powell: page 73 (bottom right)
Royal Flying Doctor Service, Southeastern Division: pages 71 (top), 115
Belinda Williams: page 82
Woman's Day: pages 1, 107

Random House: Colin Beard, page 123 (bottom); Chris Bell, pages 116-17; Greg Bridges, page 104 (top); Claver Carroll, pages 44-5, 56 (left), 108; Alexander Craig, pages 56 (right), 63 (top); Garry Fleming, page 16; Stuart Fox, page 10; Judith Kempen, pages 12, 18, 28 (bottom), 39, 53, 61 (top), 75 (bottom), 80-1, 126; David Kirschner, pages 47 (top), 48; Frank Knight, pages 49, 50; Mike Langford, pages 76, 99 (top), 126 (top); Gary Lewis, pages 101 (centre), 119; John McCann, pages 24 (bottom), 31, 32-33; Ron Moon, pages 8-9; Ron & Viv Moon, pages 4 (background), 47 (bottom); Nick Rains, page 121 (top); Rob Reichenfeld, page 27; Christo Reid, page 11 (top); Jamie Robertson, pages 22-23; Kevin Stead, page 26; Ken Stepnell, pages 30, 79, 101 (bottom); Oliver Strewe, pages 121 (centre), 122 (bottom); Murray White, page 74; James Young, pages 120, 122 (top)

Disclaimer: All possible care has been taken to make full acknowledgement for all copyright materials included. Any information that will enable the publisher to rectify any error or omission in subsequent editions is welcome.

Book signings are a great way to meet people!